unspOiLed.

This book is dedicated to all those—human,
animal, plant—who will be adversely affected
by the British Petroleum oil spill catastrophe in
the Gulf of Mexico. May we guide our leaders
towards a deeper wisdom that reflects the
interconnectedness of all beings and that puts the
health of the planet before the wealth of a few.

Cover art by David Moynahan
Artwork by David Moynahan
Book Design by Lou Cross

ISBN   978-0-9759339-1-6

Printed in the United States of America
First Printing, 06/2010

Printed on Recycled Paper, 10% post-consumer, FSC certified

Printed at Gandy Printers in Tallahassee, FL
www.gandyprinters.com

10 11 12 13 14   5 4 3 2 1

unspOiLed.

Writers Speak
for Florida's Coast

Edited by
Susan Cerulean, Janisse Ray,
and A. James Wohlpart

Artwork by
David Moynahan

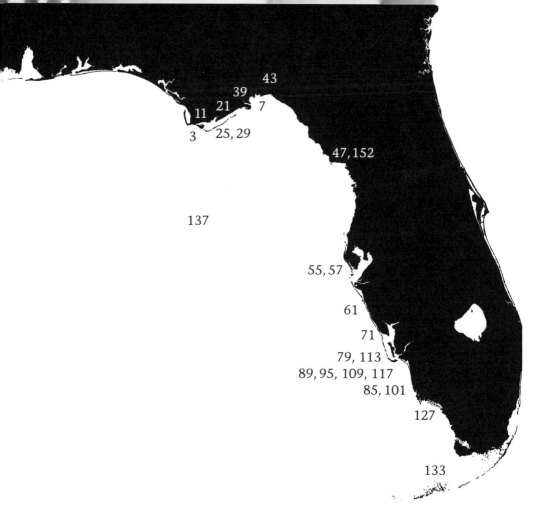

43

39

11 21   7

3   25, 29

47, 152

137

55, 57

61

71

79, 113

89, 95, 109, 117

85, 101

127

133

Map indicates page numbers of essays featuring specific locations in Florida.

CONTENTS

Site of Deepwater Horizon drilling rig
before sinking on April 22, 2010.

0   10   20 miles

SOURCE: WASHINGTON POST - MAY 11, 2010

INTRODUCTION

For nearly thirty years, our state has stood firm against oil and gas drilling off Florida shores.

As one Chamber of Commerce director said in 2008, "We have everything to lose and nothing to gain. Nothing. Drilling is not going to change the price of gas today, next week, next month, or next year. It's just going to destroy a beautiful location."

Nevertheless, in spring 2010, state legislators, underwritten by a cadre of lobbyists, public relations firms and paid pollsters, began to push hard to nullify the long-standing law protecting our Gulf of Mexico and open it to oil and gas drilling.

In November of 2009, we invited dozens of writers and poets who share our love of the Gulf to donate a short piece to this anthology we call *Unspoiled: Writers Speak for Florida's Coast*. We hoped our love of our place, and our intimacy with its wonders, unique in all the world, would infuse the public conversation with more heart and soul, and less talk of money.

We urgently hoped—we still hope—to stir ourselves from oil dependency to community resilience in the face of peak oil, climate change and economic instability.

Thirty-eight writers made time to craft impassioned essays, poems, and short fiction. Some are students, some are scientists, many are well-known Florida writers. They hail from the Panhandle to the Keys and range in age from seventy-two to just nine years old. As you will discover, our writers know well this Gulf of Mexico and the coast that cradles it, and they love it fiercely.

We also invited colleagues in several states already damaged and despoiled by offshore drilling to offer their perspectives. Readers will want to pay special attention to the cautionary tales from Alaska and Mississippi, as well as a resounding success story from North Carolina's Outer Banks.

Five months after we sent out a call for writers to speak out against drilling and to speak for our coast, we face the worst ever environmental disaster in the Gulf of Mexico. British Petroleum's spill of untold millions of gallons of oil into the Gulf was never supposed to happen, according to industry experts. But it did. And regardless of where the visible slick and tarballs make landfall, the effects on creatures that live in the Gulf are already at potentially catastrophic levels, as are the seafood and tourism industries.

We have been promised, over and over again, that drilling for oil is safe, that the state-of-the-art technology so greatly reduces the potential for oil leaks that we no longer need to be concerned about any environmental issues. We have been fed lies in the form of promises so that a few already wealthy individuals can get wealthier. We know now, with the Deepwater Horizon oil already spoiling large swaths of the Gulf of Mexico and its coast, that these lies are not to be believed. We can no longer allow the greed of a few to drive the energy and environmental decisions that affect all of us.

Even with the newest technologies and even if there were no spills, oil companies still legally pollute by dumping drilling muds and other toxic fluids into the waters surrounding their rigs. These wastes are laden with heavy metals, carcinogens, and radioactive materials. Each platform also legally spews greenhouse gases and pollutants into the air. And every year, there are oil spills and blowouts somewhere in the world.

The late nineteenth century and the entire twentieth century have been closely intertwined with the story of petroleum and the benefits and consequences of its use. The economic fortunes to be made from oil evoked a frenzy of exploration, especially after the invention of the gasoline-powered automobile and airplane. The petroleum industry has become the world's most profitable, supporting everything from agriculture to plastics to transportation, and is undoubtedly the central feature of the world's economy. Eminent cultural historian Thomas Berry wrote, "We are so conditioned by our dependence on petroleum and its benefits that we can hardly imagine life without those benefits."

The amount of petroleum present on Earth is immense, but eventually it will be exhausted. For this reason, governments all over the world backed by powerful multinational corporations are overpowering the wishes of their citizens and risking more and more environmental damage to mine what fossil fuel remains. We in

Florida who wish to preserve the integrity of our turquoise Gulf are fighting the same battle as West Virginians or Kentuckians outraged by the mountaintop removal of coal or Canadians witnessing the enormous damage perpetrated by the extraction of oil from shale. And all of us are fighting the climate crisis, which is fueled by our petroleum-dependent economy.

Thomas Berry foresaw that the story of the twenty-first century will be the "story of the terminal phase of petroleum, and the invention of new patterns of human living in relation to Earth's resources in the post-petroleum period." So, as oil chokes sea turtles and bluefin tuna, plankton and oysters and fish larvae, and eventually washes up on the beaches of our coast, we face a stark choice about our energy future. Will we respond in ways deep enough to matter, or will we continue on a path of destruction and dirty energy? Can we help our people and our leaders understand the depth of our addiction to the fossil fuel? Will we continue to think that we must choose between a clean and healthy environment and energy use? Will we build a movement that's powerful enough to push us onto the path of a clean energy future?

We believe in the power of our artists and writers and naturalists to help guide us in this time when desperation and greed have come disguised as virtues. Our story is deeply intertwined with the story of this place, this Florida coast that we all—Democrat and Republican, liberal and conservative—have worked so diligently to protect. To speak for Florida coastal waters is an act of faith, a belief that hope will prevail over desperation, that good sense will trump greed.

We have returned to a time when we speak with one voice across Florida, when we can share what we love most about our beaches and our waters in ways that resonate loudly with the imagination and dreams of many Floridians. We believe that we can come together once again to share what we love most, to protect it, and to open ourselves to its wild nature.

—*Susan Cerulean, Janisse Ray, and A. James Wohlpart*

unspOiLed.

FIRST LANDFALL

JANISSE RAY

I am almost forty-eight years old, in what I hope is the middle of my life, walking a remote path on the east side of a wild barrier island, Gulf of Mexico, Florida. The day is in early January, and I am celebrating a new year where bald eagles nest, where red wolves have been reintroduced, where migratory birds land and feed after their long journeys, and where signs of Native American habitation, mostly oyster-shell middens, still abound.

Friends and I boated here this morning, across Indian Pass to a protected inlet with 360 degrees of wildness except for one oyster boat easing through Saint Vincent Sound, toward Apalachicola Bay. I walked alone around a spit and down a beach that faces the morning sun, keeping to a strand firmed by outgoing tide.

I can't remember being on a beach more wild. I pause to examine sand dollars and sponges. Sometimes uprooted trees, eroding majestically in wind and tide, block the way. I walk backwards against the calendar, against the years, becoming the young woman I have been, who had time for nature, who did not sit for long hours at a desk—and on backwards toward the naturalist and the explorer and then the native I do not remember being, although the ancient landscape stirs in me reminders.

My friends and I are the only people, I am sure, on this wild January island, and now I am almost a mile from my friends, down a wild beach.

But the wild island can only be as wild as the Gulf that surrounds it, and the Gulf can't get away from people. Around me the beach is littered with human detritus—plastic buckets, Styrofoam crab floats, rubber gloves from the oystermen, plastic drink bottles, aluminum cans. Part of a dock has washed ashore, treated lumber with nails exposed. A boat passes and I hear its deckhands calling to each other.

The things we manufacture and use away from this wild refuge wind up here anyway, in the one place they should not be. I stand and look out at the Gulf, my head full of terrible thoughts, thinking about an oil spill and what would happen to this place, warm Gulf waters unswimmable, beach contaminated, sea life extinguished. The thought of it is too horrendous to dwell upon. The worst of human civilization insinuates itself in the best of what we have left.

I see a woods path and go inland. I am far, far away from everything I don't like about the world, and I am in the embrace of that which I love most.

The maritime forest is alive with magnolia and live oak, with tall cabbage palms. This is not a thin forest, not a sparse forest, not a new forest, not a forest to be taken lightly. This is an old forest on an old barrier island where red wolves have been calling.

As I walk I am remembering the young woman I used to be, who came alive in wind and sun.

These feelings are especially strong because the Gulf of Mexico was the territory in which I came of age. Here I first saw plovers nesting on beach sand. Here I saw a freshwater spring bubbling from the salty depths of the Gulf. Here I experienced wildfire. Here I made my first bird list and retrieved my first scallop, caught my first shark. Here I tasted smoked mullet and found an ancient pottery shard and sailed and identified an oystercatcher. Here, as I said, I came alive.

As I walk I am making resolutions. As I walk I am coming back from the dead.

In the New Year, outside will be inside. I will spend more nights out of doors, the way I used to do. I will canoe more rivers. I will celebrate the high holidays of the sun, earth's calendar, with ceremonies that involve fire and no money. I will pay more attention to birds.

I will use less, stay home more. I will think about the consequences of my decisions on even the smallest menhaden in the sea.

Along my path are the large bones of sambar deer. In an owl pellet (marked by white stains on leaves, below a level branch) I poke around and find the tiny skull of a rodent. I am happy in these old coastal woods, happy in the middle of my life, happy in this moment.

Writer, naturalist, and activist Janisse Ray is author of three books of literary nonfiction. Ray resided in the Florida Panhandle from 1982 to 1995 and now attempts to live a simple, sustainable life on a farm in southern Georgia with her husband, Raven Waters. She coedited, with Susan Cerulean and Laura Newton, Between Two Rivers: Stories from the Red Hills to the Gulf. *She has been a scholar-in-residence at Florida Gulf Coast University and was awarded an honorary doctorate from Unity College in Maine.*

FLORIDA POSTCARD

JULIE HAUSERMAN

The butterflies are so fragile. I can't stop thinking about them as I sit at the State Capitol and listen to the men in suits talk money, talk deals.

I never knew that the monarch's wings are made of clear webbing with orange and black dust. To put a tiny tag on the butterfly, I have to rub a little of the color off its wing. Then I stick on a miniscule tag and set the butterfly free. I watch it teeter off on the sea wind towards Central America.

It's a bit of an improbable experiment, tagging butterflies on the clean, bright Panhandle coast, hoping somebody across the Gulf of Mexico will find a beautiful dead insect, pick it up, and call the number on the teensy tag to tell us where it lands. But this is how we are trying to quantify their mysterious, awesome journey.

Scientists tell us only one in a thousand monarchs makes it from the wintering grounds in Mexico back to the Florida coast. They move across America to Canada in waves of birth and death. The seventh generation makes it home to Canada. The butterflies have been making this flight for millions of years, over these turquoise waves and this old, sandy shore.

At the front of the room, the men in suits are making a hideous promise to Florida legislators. The money from their dirty oil rigs, they propose with hopeful faces, can go to conservation programs! They will actually be saving Florida! It's a slick bargain that makes the lawmakers look up from their Blackberries.

Except. The Panhandle sand is famous, blindingly perfect, out of this world and in it. We are living the Florida postcard. Our kids toddle to the waves, make drip castles, chase gulls. Our grandparents sit under wide-brimmed hats, listening to the surf. Our dogs dig ghost crabs under the full moon.

Why on earth would we gamble on wrecking a place where butterflies linger, where crabs skitter and dolphins prowl? The *Exxon Valdez* spill happened twenty years ago, and still people can stick shovels in the Alaska shoreline and expose black oil. We dig down into Florida's sandy beach and find arrowheads and ancient shells, and we pull them up into the sunshine, lucky us.

When I am on a Panhandle beach, the sugar sand I sift with my toes is 5 million years old, quartz crystals sorted and carried by water and wind. So clean, it squeaks when I walk. We never had sand like this where I came from, up north. I could hardly believe it the first time I saw it; it looked fake. Now I see these dunes in my dreams, in a love affair with this coast that's two decades strong.

Once, when I was deeply troubled and walking the bone-white beach, I found a trail of small bird feathers, attractive with two white dots on black. Every time I picked one up, my thoughts gained clarity. At the end of the trail, I had a pocket full of feathers and a solution that moved my life forward. The beach is like that. It gives us time to breathe, it gives us the rare gift of perspective in our scurrying lives.

In our postcard, black skimmers with gaudy orange

clown beaks build a nest right on the beach. The nest is nothing more than a wispy scrape on the bare sugar surface, as delicate as a monarch's wing. I like to lie quietly in the early morning beach fog, flat against the sand, and enter the shorebird world, waves rocking, tiny legs moving in a blur, crabs fleeing for their lives.

We are so blessed.

The oil lobbyists whisper pretty lies in the lawmakers' ears, hand over fat checks, they praise and bow to power. They are good at what they do, as relentless as sharks chasing prey in gray winter waves.

I want to stand up here in this windowless Capitol room and tell them they can't buy our postcard, no matter how much money they flash in their fat wallets. I want us all to circle like dolphins and run them off.

Julie Hauserman has been writing about Florida's environment for twenty-three years. She was a Capitol bureau reporter for the St. Petersburg Times *and an essayist for National Public Radio's* Weekend Edition-Sunday *and* The Splendid Table. *Her work is featured in several Florida anthologies, including* The Wild Heart of Florida, The Book of the Everglades, *and* Between Two Rivers: Stories from the Red Hills to the Gulf.

MULLET RUN

SUSAN CERULEAN

The egg of a mullet is a tiny thing, smaller than the point of a pencil, yet filled with the purpose of becoming fish. Mother mullet bear over a half million such ova, transparent and tinted the color of straw. In the heart of each egg lies a single, buoyant globule of oil.

In no way does this perfectly contained oil, so necessary in just this quantity to the life of the fish (which we may someday eat), resemble the petroleum that has spewed by the millions of gallons from a criminally, carelessly installed and leaking pipeline off Louisiana's coast.

For a mullet egg to grow into a fish, the parents and their offspring require the whole range of our coastal waters. In the clean deep Gulf, mullet spawn and lay their eggs, which transform and grow into larvae. Then, through the inlets and passes, the young larvae swim to salt creeks and marshes to fatten and grow.

One winter morning, my husband Jeff and I stood by a pass near Apalachicola and watched the water come twitching alive with mullet, and we saw for ourselves their essential journey. There weren't many at first, but within minutes, the fish coalesced by the thousands into broad riffling rafts that wheeled slowly past us into the Gulf.

I'm used to the leap of a mullet or two at a time, but I'd never seen anything like this rich press of fish. My husband ran for his cast net.

"It's a run!" called a nearby fisherman, throwing his own net from the beach. "The males are up here on top, and the females are deeper under the water—spawning."

Driven by the night's projected temperatures, near freezing, all these thousands of mullet were headed offshore towards the Gulf's still warm waters. The man had guessed the run was coming. He said he had seen two acres of mullet in the lagoon back behind the pass the day before, but it was too shallow to get in there after them with a boat.

Jeff hauled in his net. Eight or nine keepers in just one cast. I loosened the fish from the net, stilled their bodies between my palms, and shelved them in our cooler.

Presently a dozen or more local dolphins arrived, and neither the mullet nor the dolphins cared anything about us, or our whirling nets, or how far out we waded.

The dolphins handled the fish into a tight panicked circle the size of half a tennis court. For just a moment, the big animals shoved the mullet almost to our beach with powerful thrusting arcs of their bodies, then herded them right back out into the pass, more like armed guards than Flipper.

Word of the mullet run was out. A handful of fishing skiffs with three and four men apiece launched at the ramp and powered into the phenomenal frenzy of fish, dolphins and plunging pelicans. From their boats, they threw short-braille nets weighted with chain-link, which were made, like ours, by a man named Charlie out of Port St. Joe. The fishermen whooped and hollered. We could hear the heavy bodies of their captives thunk against the metal bottoms of the boats. They tossed back the smaller, sleeker white roe males, filling their coolers only with red-roe bearing females. I heard one man speculate that he'd get thirty cents a pound for white roe, considerably more for red. He was thinking pounds of fish translated into dollars at the market later that day.

Cold winter air began to bear down on the pass from the north. The weather had been changing over us all day long, a sprinkle, some sun, another stretch of cloud.

I fetched my fillet knife and a white plastic cutting board, and cleaned four of our fish for dinner. The female was a good third larger and heavier than the males. Her roe—the eggs of new life short-stopped by our net—lay like enormous orange sausages in her abdominal cavity. More egg than flesh in this female who had intended to spawn offshore tonight.

Out in the pass, the three boats of anglers returned again and again to the ramp, unloading their coolers into their trucks. It was hard not to get caught up in the moment of utter plenty. Even the two of us, our cooler crammed with fish, considered launching our own boat to join the others in the pass. But we had already caught all the mullet we could eat or give away to friends.

"How often do you see a run like this?" I called over to a man working alone in a flatbottom metal skiff with a 40-horsepower Mercury motor.

"Once a year," he said. "I was cat fishing on the river when I got the call. I had shot me three squirrels, but I came on over here as quick I could when I heard about the run." He wore a tomato red sweatshirt and brown khakis, looked to be in his 60s. He told us he was the volunteer fire chief from Apalachicola. He struggled alone with his skiff, the motor, his net, and the swift tide, but he was really happy. "This is the most fish I've ever caught in my life. If I catch enough, I'll have a benefit fish fry for the department."

Later, Jeff and I sat in our warm little rented cottage on

the hill, using forks and then our fingers, to dig the thick and sweet backbone meat straight off a pan we'd carried in from the grill. We had butterfly-filleted the mullet, then grilled it in a little foil boat with butter and plenty of fresh pressed garlic.

Out in the dusk, I could see that the chief was the last man on the pass, still throwing that net. I wished I'd asked him how many fish it takes to hold a fund-raising fry.

Writer, gardener, and activist Susan Cerulean's nature memoir, Tracking Desire: A Journey after Swallow-tailed Kites *was an* Audubon *magazine Editors' Choice. Cerulean finds satisfaction in bringing together collaborative groups of writers and artists to sing praises and sound alarm on behalf of her place on Earth. She is at work on a book about the coastal islands of the Florida Panhandle.*

SELLING FLORIDA

DIANE ROBERTS

Forget, for a moment, the environmental argument. Forget that the beaches of the Gulf of Mexico could be ruined, the powdered-sugar sand gone slick and black with outlaw crude. Forget the turquoise waves stained with oil. Forget the dying fish, the pelicans and gulls blinded and poisoned by tar. Forget all that beauty doomed. Let's talk money.

Lots of money. Serious revenue enhancement. *Mucho dinero.* Orlando economist and drilling advocate Hank Fishkind says that authorizing the exploration and production of near-shore oil and natural gas reserves could have Florida fat with cash: between $2.2 billion a year to as much as $12 billion a year. Drilling in the Gulf will create twenty thousand new jobs—maybe even more.

Damn, that sounds sweet, what with our 11 percent unemployment, our declining population, and our anorexic budgets. Other states drill in the Gulf: why not us?

Florida could be just like Texas, Louisiana, and Alabama, raking in the royalty dollars. So says Florida Energy Associates, the people who hired Dr. Fishkind, the people hollering "drill here, drill now." One of their spokesmodels, one M. Lance Phillips of Mexia, Texas, a lawyer and self-described "oil man," insists that Florida's future energy earnings "can literally fund everything Florida wants to do."

Everything we want to do! How great would that be? We could have the best schools in the nation: no more overcrowded classrooms (no need to spend money repealing that pesky amendment), no more outdated textbooks, no more underpaid teachers. Our social services, brimming with petro-dollars, would care for all our sick and elderly, and look after all our vulnerable children. Our courts, properly funded for the first time in years, could dispense justice in a timely manner. Our universities, transported from the bottom of the appropriations food chain, could refurbish their libraries, hire more faculty, and give scholarships to more students; our streets would be safe, because of all those new cops on the beat; the Everglades would be protected (we'd simply buy back all that land—chump change to oil billionaires like us). Culturally, there'd be so much moola around, Florida would remind everyone of Florence in the age of Leonardo. Our roads would be in perfect shape, smooth as a baby's fanny, and our gasoline would be so cheap we could have a different Hummer for every day of the week. Just like Texas, Louisiana, and Alabama!

Except (this is a *little* awkward), despite their oil, Texas, Louisiana, and Alabama have not been transformed. These states are known for many things (quality football, great barbecue, brilliant musicians) but enlightened state governments, resources lavishly expended on the welfare of their citizens, or a justice system that's anything to write home about? Is it possible oil earnings ain't all they're cracked up to be?

Texas, Louisiana, and Alabama all rank in the bottom fifth nationally in per pupil spending (just like Florida). The energy industry has not cured their job problems: Texas has

8.2 percent unemployment, while Louisiana's is 8 percent. Alabama's is the same as Florida's: 11 percent. Oil money hasn't solved their states' environmental issues or taken care of their poor and ailing or fixed their highways and bridges. Oil money has not lifted the level of culture up to that of Periclean Athens—or even Athens, Georgia (though I admit Austin is pretty cool). Compared to Florida, gasoline is indeed a little cheaper on average in Alabama and Texas: about eight cents per gallon. Louisiana runs about six cents per gallon less than in Florida. Not enough to make filling up those big rides a bargain.

In October 2009, a *St. Petersburg Times* editorial pointed out that Alabama makes between $50 million and $300 million from oil royalties and Texas gets around $45 million a year. Nothing like the big bucks promised to Florida. They already know where "their" oil is: they should just be raking it in, shouldn't they? We don't know, first, where the oil in Florida's waters might be, and, second, if there is any oil in the first place.

As Stephen Colbert might say, "Damn you, Logic!"

Nevertheless, the Drill Team at Florida Energy Associates insists that extracting "our" oil is the best hope for a return to the good times of cheap gas and full coffers. And to encourage Florida citizens (and, more importantly, Florida legislators) to embrace drilling here and drilling now, Florida Energy Associates has hired three dozen lobbyists. One of their lobbyists is Claudia Diaz de la Portilla, who is (what a coincidence!) married to Alex Diaz de la Portilla, senate majority leader and (another coincidence!) chairman of the Energy, Environment, and Land Use Committee.

Well, now we know who you have to sleep with to get Florida's ban on drilling repealed.

But wait, there's more—more money even than hiring an army of lobbyists, I mean. Florida Energy Associates has made a down payment of $75,000 to the Florida Republican Party and $50,000 to the Florida Democratic Party. This is soft money, which means it's practically unlimited. They can (and will) contribute much more. And they don't even have to say who they are! As Carl Hiaasen said, "That's what makes our legislators so special. They happily sell out without even knowing who's buying them."

So Florida Energy Associates is veiled in secrecy, faceless, incognito. But they're not, according to Doug Daniels, a Daytona Beach lawyer, "shadowy." Daniels, another hired gun, says they just want to protect their "competitive advantage." Just business, you know. Mr. Daniels says that once the drilling ban is repealed, they'll go public, since the application to drill opposite your favorite beach requires real names.

Still, many of us would just feel a little more comfortable if we knew who the new owners of our state government were. Are they backed by big oil? Exxon? (Great record in Alaska.) Shell? (Check out the Niger Delta.) Are they marginal outfits, really out to greenmail the state into buying back leases for a tidy profit? For all we know Florida Energy Associates could be the Skull and Bones Club or Opus Dei or maybe even the Church of Scientology (hey, at least they're local). So far, all we've got is Daniels and M. Lance Phillips. The *St. Pete Times* found out that Mr. Phillips is a big-game hunter and friends with former president George W. Bush and indicted Texas fraudster R. Allen Stanford. If that's not sufficiently reassuring, Mr. Daniels says Mr. Phillips comes "from a good Texas family."

This would be great if he wanted to pledge Sigma Nu, but seeing as he wants to endanger our $60 billion tourist industry, we need a little more in the way of hard facts. Remember, we're talking money here.

Here's the thing about Florida and money. Other states sell stuff they make (widgets, cogs), stuff they grow (corn, cotton), or stuff they think up (dot.coms, insurance). Florida sells itself. *Come live in tropical warmth, palm-treed beauty, low-tax condo paradise.* Is drilling a draw for snowbirds? Maybe we could market an adventure holiday scrubbing spilled oil off sea birds on Florida's Gulf Coast.

So we're going to lash our economic future to a dirty industry that fosters the fantasy that we can keep burning fossil fuels forever—or until the last Escalade leaves the lot? If Florida lawmakers truly want to find a new way to fund the state (and, given revenue projections, that would be a really good idea), why not go for the estimated ninety thousand jobs that could be created in renewable energy? You don't have to drill for sunlight; you don't need a pipeline to transport the wind. If we know nothing else, those of us who have lived in Florida more than five minutes know this: nature is more powerful than the latest technology. We will have hurricanes, tornadoes, floods. And more and more, the sea, swollen by melting ice far away, is rising. Florida, the last of North America to emerge from the water, will be the first to return.

Diane Roberts is an eighth generation Floridian, author of Dream State, *commentator for National Public Radio, and Professor of Creative Writing at Florida State University. Her work appears in the* Washington Post, *the* Times of London, *and the* St. Petersburg Times.

KEEPING WATCH

DAWN EVANS RADFORD

A descendant of local lighthouse keepers, I consider my greatest blessing my childhood years growing up on Florida's Panhandle, where life presented itself to me naturally graceful and colorfully rich. Estuaries teemed with beds of silky, succulent oysters across Apalachicola Bay, nurseries of shrimp and blue crab in estuarine marshes, and rare grass beds for spawning mullet, trout, sturgeon, and the leviathan-like tarpon. Black bears and manatees shared habitat with alligators and ospreys; orchids and pitcher plants grew alongside giant oaks and dwarf cypress. Now after decades of living and traveling over the globe, I have come to cherish the magical beauty and veritable treasure trove of diversity thriving in this corner of Florida.

On a recent trip to the Galapagos, I marveled at my first glimpse of blue feet on booby birds. I watched a giant tortoise cross a stony pasture, photographed a male frigatebird cuddling his snowball-white chick, climbed volcanoes, and straddled the equator. I took note of the care with which the Ecuadorian government oversees these islands, care which makes possible the presentation of the Galapagos as a monument to nature, attracting multiple millions of tourists and scientists year-round.

Yet upon return to the Panhandle my heart melted at the sight of birds in and over the Apalachicola Bay at Carrabelle, more variety of birds in one glance than I had seen in an entire week on the Galapagos. The following morning, I counted more types of birds, butterflies, and flowers on my humble Florida acre than on all the Galapagos Islands combined.

Other travels have carried me to UNESCO sites around the world. Among my favorites have been world heritage villages in Dominica and Thailand. UNESCO World Heritage programs protect and celebrate special places and cultures which may have been lost without this attention. In Dominica's and Thailand's UNESCO villages, descendants of indigenous people live and work in communities like those of their ancient forebears. These villages serve their countries and the concerned global public as open, living museums in their original settings, of authentic charm and memorial, educating and entertaining, as well as providing lucrative tourist destinations.

Upon returning home from these sites, I looked about me at several of our own distinctive qualifications as potential sites of world heritage: our historical seafood industry and the dependent subculture which developed along with it from the very earliest settling of Florida's human inhabitants. I felt twice blessed to have such history and heritage.

In the early twentieth century, the mystique of the Panhandle appealed to my grandfather, lighthouse keeper at Cape San Blas and later bridge tender at the river entrance to Apalachicola. He passed his last days on the water fishing and oystering, and on his half acre tending flowers and vegetables. He left to me his love of the fruitful land and water here, and his concern that we tend to our surroundings with the same care as if they were a UNESCO World Heritage site. He would agree that we Floridians share stewardship of the resources and promise of the Panhandle, as well as of numerous other comely corners of Florida. We cannot afford to gamble the treasure we hold in our hands for that which some few *might* gain if nothing goes awry with bonanzas in the Gulf.

Raised in the Florida Panhandle, Dawn Evans Radford has published poetry, literary research, and fiction, including a novel, Oyster Flats, *set in the Panhandle. Winner of the 1993 Sherwood Anderson Award, she lives in Franklin County where she is currently at work on a second novel.*

ONCE MORE TO THE COAST

ERIN CANTER

The brilliant summer sun follows a group of friends as we drive along the Gulf coast to Saint George Island from Tallahassee. We wind along, windows down, arms outstretched, music humming lightly in our ears. Slash pines race past us, and beyond them, a hazy littoral scene emerges as though on an old film, shaking and spinning with the reel. Pelicans perch on wooden posts protruding from the soft saline waters. Wading fishermen cast their lines and nets and reel in the day's catch.

My friends and I have no plan or schedule, and this does not perturb us; we have each other and a seemingly unlimited supply of Florida's stunning coast. But we are impatient by the time we slow to a stop at the entrance gate at the state park. Eager to see the beauty protected beyond, we quickly shovel out equal portions of the entrance fee. Our pent-up energy is finally set free as we spill out of the car and canter over the boardwalk for our first look at the ocean.

The snow-white beaches burn our bare feet and we dash to the water for relief. The clear Gulf becomes the backdrop for our knee-deep Frisbee games, volleyball competitions, and general summer shenanigans. The sun drains our energy, and eventually we fall in a comfortable exhaustion into the white foam along the water's edge.

The sanderlings outlast us, and we watch them scamper along the shoreline as we recline in the shallow water. We make salty drip castles on our knees while we wait for the sun to set. Even after the sea gulls and children cease their laughter and the dunes turn to shadows which then turn to darkness, the ever-present lull of breaking waves continues its sweet rhythm.

Darkness flows over us, following the pattern of the breeze that drifts seaward. Lights fade and then disappear completely. Tiny hard-shelled sea turtles will not be confused if they hatch tonight and make their first shuffles in the sand, joining their brethren in the dark water. What a night to be born.

The Milky Way wanders in a sleepy haze across the domed sky. We lie on our backs, a tangle of teenagers gazing upward and outward, irrationally yet undeniably empowered as the infinite sky casts starlight on our infinitesimal bodies. There is no separation between the water's deep darkness and the sky it gently reflects. We happily succumb to disorientation. The sky never ends, and we let ourselves believe that our surroundings, too, are constant.

In such bliss it's easy to forget that this sanctuary is fragile. That this island, protected by the title of State Park and a minor fee, is by definition surrounded by water, a substance as beautiful in its purity as it is endangered by degradation. To preserve this moment, this day, this unforgettable experience, we have to protect what surrounds our haven. Without exchanging a word, my friends and I share the understanding that nothing is worth defacing Florida's coast.

We will come back to this beach, to this coast, to this

Gulf, forever expecting the beauty of the day and the power of the night. We are cradled by the warmth of our convictions, just as the Florida coast is cradled by the warm embrace of the Gulf Stream that flows along her curves.

Erin Canter grew up and continues to live around the forests and waters of north Florida. An avid traveler, Erin speaks three languages and enjoys exploring other countries as well as her own. She is currently studying environmental science and linguistics.

THE SHINING GULF

CRYSTAL WAKOA

Drought had a chokehold on Tallahassee. The national forest south of town burned out of control most of June. With an evening thunderstorm threatening the festivities at Tom Brown Park, Saint George Island seemed a safer bet for fireworks this Fourth of July. God knows my daughter and I needed an outing.

"Nice to breathe some fresh air, huh, honey?" I said, watching Lumin stick her feet out the car window as we cruised the familiar route from Tallahassee to Saint George: Panacea, Ochlocknee Bay, Saint Teresa, Carrabelle, each town like a native wildflower—hardy, singular, lovely— leading us to the ragged bloom of Eastpoint, fragrant with the briny scent of so many memories spent at the beloved beach across the bridge.

In my mind's eye I pictured fireworks shot high over the Gulf, but a hand-painted sign directed us to the bay side of the island. We parked at Harry A's bar and walked back down the road to the growing crowd claiming space with their blankets on the thin strip of flat, scruffy shoreline sprouting marsh grass and sea oats, affording a fine view of the sky above Apalachicola Bay.

A battered pick-up with five "Save Our Seafood" stickers plastered across its bumper slowed next to us, spilling a leathered, middle-aged woman and four young kids who wasted no time running down the shoreline yelling and waving old-fashioned pinwheels. We settled on our quilt at the edge of the crowd, scaring a fiddler crab off into the marsh grass. Four shirtless teenage boys in blue jean cutoffs ambled by, sneaking peeks at Lumin, her arms wrapped around her legs, chin on knees, thick blonde curls rolling down her back. Masquerading as any aloof sixteen-year-old, she was quietly tending her broken heart, having said her last goodbye to her dad who had died just seven days earlier. Lumin's dad and I had been apart for a decade, but I was present at his death—an unexpected healing for both of us.

Cars and trucks streamed across the bridge in a steady flow. A ruddy-faced man with tattooed arms shouted, "It's stormin' in Tallahassee! They shut down Tom Brown Park!" A couple with a toddler atop the dad's shoulders walked by just as the little girl dropped her lollipop into her dad's scraggly long hair, coaxing a chuckle out of Lumin. I took in the crowd with a state of mind sharpened by death's aftermath, holding all things precious and quivering in their ordinariness, feeling the fragility of our tiny family of two buoyed up among this swelling sea of families.

Sparklers lit up at dusk, then inexplicably stopped too soon. People began packing up their blankets and coolers and walking back to their cars.

Absorbed in watchful moods, we listened as the crowd passed by.

"I dunno, Pumpkin. Fire marshal must've called it off."

"We'll see fireworks next year, hon. It's okay. Hurry up, now."

"Stop teasing your sister, Matt."

One of the last to leave, a large man in a fluorescent orange t-shirt waved to Lumin and me, exclaiming, "Nothin's for sure! Never know what's comin' or what ain't!"

"Not much is for sure, that's for sure!" I hailed back.

Lumin leaned into me as we watched the ribbon of tail lights recede across the bridge.

"What's for sure, Mom?" she asked with a heartbreaking mix of challenge and sorrow.

Knowing the enormity of her loss would take years to unravel, I gathered myself to tell her . . . what? That love, the bare bones truth of impermanence, life's moment-to-moment richness and the piercing beauty of this world, all that sustained us, was present in that very moment, the two of us awash in the fading pink of summer sky over the bay?

"Want to go to our beach?" I asked instead.

She softened and nodded, and we drove over the body of Saint George to the Gulf of Mexico and headed west to the state park at the end of the island. We parked at the entrance, closed since dusk, and walked the sandy path to the beach in the growing dark. A waxing moon, three quarters full, lit our way.

"Wow, Mama, look!" Lumin stopped in her tracks in front of me as the surf came into view. Phosphorescence twinkled and sparked on the forward crests of wave after gentle wave. We stood there, entranced by the starry seascape, an ocean of fireflies, a jazz riff of liquid light.

"Tiny sea creatures turning their energy into light," I whispered.

"We get to see fireworks after all," Lumin responded in wonderment.

We sat on the cool, white sand at the edge of the surf in the deepening dark. A decade of memories anchored us there: birthday parties, kite flying, body surfing, sand sculpting, beach combing, long walks and endless hours swimming in the clear, clean Gulf.

The surf pulsed and spread before us. I lay back, wiggled my hips into the sand, but Lumin was up, pulling my wrist. "C'mon, Mama, let's go in."

The water was cool against our legs. We waded in together, scooped at the phosphorescence that sifted through our fingers, refusing to be caught. And then she was off. Lumin dove and came up splashing me, teasing me in, her face lit up like I hadn't seen in months.

We swam out to the calm water and floated on our backs together under the shining moon.

Crystal Wakoa is a psychotherapist and writer who lives in Wakulla County, Florida.

BIG OIL, BIG SIN

CONNIE MAY FOWLER

Florida. You know it, right? This sand bar of a state graced with sugar sand beaches and cerulean waters; the singularly beautiful stretch of *terra firma* where one can sit on the shoreline and gaze at the unbroken union of sea and sky; a holy habitat, really, where dolphin and manatee, heron and eagle, sea turtle and starfish move in time to the ancient rhythms of celestial bodies.

Three miles out. That's where Big Oil wants to place their rigs. And because they are trying to create cover for the politicians who might very well vote this insanity into law, they have actually stated that the accoutrements that accompany the drilling process are "virtually invisible." Folks, we've elected legislators who actually believe in invisible oil rigs.

According to a November 29, 2009, article in the *Sarasota Herald-Tribune* written by Jeremy Wallace, even their "drill, baby, drill" brethren aren't buying the lie. Mr. Wallace writes: "Oil industry officials scoff at the notion of a virtually invisible rig. Denise McCourt, industry relations director for the American Petroleum Institute, said recovering oil from the ocean requires traditional fixed platforms or a pipeline infrastructure like the one around Louisiana and Texas, where drilling has been going on since the 1940s. 'There's no such thing as an invisible rig,' McCourt said."

Lest we forget, repeat after me, pro-drillers: There's no such thing as an invisible rig.

In the spirit of total disclosure, I have something in common with our oil-grubbing enemies: I can be greedy too. In addition to the wholly nightmarish prospect of oil derricks sprouting like metal vultures from the blue waters of the Gulf and new refineries mushrooming in toxic glory amid our marshlands, drilling would toll the death knell for Florida's $60 billion recreation and tourism industry. Phil Compton pointed out in a July 24, 2009, article in Tampa's *Creative Loafing*, "If you were here in the early '90s, you'll remember a relatively tiny oil spill from a tanker accident. Result: In two years Pinellas County tourism dropped 45 percent, losing about $5 billion dollars in 2008 dollars."

That's what Big Oil wants us to do: destroy a perfectly good economic engine that, while it has its faults, is relatively eco-friendly and benefits a large portion of our population in favor of one that will destroy the environment and benefit almost no one. And that's where my greed comes in. I want more people to make more money while saving more of the ecosystem. How crazy is that?

Forget that we are on the cusp of discovering and inventing alternative energy sources that will not only make offshore drilling passé (an environmental Marquis de Sade joke) but might very well save the planet.

Forget future-think: keep us pinned to the mistake-riddled past so that we remain dependent on fossil fuels and, in the process, break Mother Nature's back.

Forget the truth: Even if we began drilling offshore tomorrow, we wouldn't see it affect energy prices for seven to ten years. Drilling in the Arctic National Wildlife Refuge will gain us even slower results. Let's be optimistic and roll the dice at seven. With the proper inspiration (which $4-plus a gallon gas truly is) and sound policies (investing in new technologies), surely we will develop those deeply needed alternative energy sources. Why say no to foreign oil when we should be saying no to oil, period?

Senator John McCain stated in a town hall meeting in Wisconsin during the last presidential campaign that offshore drilling was not the answer: "With those resources, which would take years to develop, you would only postpone or temporarily relieve our dependency on fossil fuels. We are going to have to go to alternative energy, and the exploitation of existing reserves of oil, natural gas, even coal, and we can develop clean coal technology, are all great things. But we also have to devote our efforts, in my view, to alternative energy sources, which is the ultimate answer to our long-term energy needs, and we need it sooner rather than later."

I know the good senator flip-flops on this issue with all the vigor of a beached mullet, but the only people that Florida offshore drilling benefits are the folks who are trying to make us believe in invisible oil rigs. Their purposes are completely at odds with the long-term welfare of our state, our country, our planet.

Big Oil also would have us believe that offshore drilling is an accident-free endeavor. But according to the International Tanker Owners Pollution Federation, between 1997 and 2007, there have been 242 spills from tankers, combined carriers, and barges (acts of war not included). On July 27, 2009, an underwater pipeline owned by Shell Pipeline cracked off the coast of Louisiana, releasing approximately 63,000 gallons of crude oil into the Gulf of Mexico. If you conduct a Google search for "oil spill gulf of mexico" you get approximately 166,000 hits.

If any of you, dear readers, have ever been to Texas City, surely you know that refineries turn the air we breathe into a lethal stew and the neighborhoods we once loved into a Hieronymus Bosch hellscape. T.S. Eliot's poem "The Wasteland" has been a favorite of mine since grade school, but I never truly understood what a wasteland was until I stumbled upon Texas City.

The other side has lots and lots of money. By and large, those of us who oppose the destruction of beautiful *La Florida* don't. But we do have lots and lots of love for this embattled jewel of a state. We might not be rich, but we can and must be stalwart in our conviction that offshore oil drilling never stains one drop of water, one grain of sand. There is no room for compromise. Simply put, drilling for oil in Florida waters must never take place.

As I write this, I am left with a familiar longing that humankind not blow asunder what nature has made. I gaze out my window at the Gulf of Mexico and am reminded of something Nick Blue says in *Remembering Blue*, my novel about the area of Florida I live in.

"I know what the Bible meant when it said God cast Adam and Eve out of paradise," he tells his wife, Mattie. "God didn't send them anywhere; he took something away. Their animal eyes, all that under the surface stuff that lets us know we're part and parcel with the beasts and fish and snakes. He turned us into fools in our own land."

Nick was being harsh on himself. He still believed in Florida as paradise. He paused, and listened, and understood that he was an ever-evolving, deeply important participant in something awesome, something that should be considered sacred: this good earth. As so many of the fisher folk in my part of the world do, Nick Blue walked the talk.

We have to take a stand. We cannot allow those who lost their animal eyes years ago to turn the rest of us into fools. May we never be so lost that we say, "Oil rig? You mean that virtually invisible monstrosity right out there? Where paradise once lay?"

Connie May Fowler is an award-winning novelist, memoirist, and screenwriter. Grand Central Publishing will publish her most recent novel, How Clarissa Burden Learned to Fly *in 2010. She is the author of* Sugar Cage, River of Hidden Dreams, The Problem with Murmur Lee, Remembering Blue *(recipient of the Chautauqua South Literary Award) and* Before Women had Wings *(recipient of the 1996 Southern Book Critics Circle Award and the Francis Buck Award from the League of American Pen Women). Her work has been translated into eighteen languages and is published worldwide. Her essays have been published in the* New York Times, London Times, International Herald Tribune, Japan Times, Oxford American, Best Life, *and elsewhere. Ms. Fowler travels the country, speaking on topics such as writing, self-employment in the arts, literacy, domestic violence, child abuse, environmental issues, and popular culture. She is a Florida native.*

LIVING FROM THE GULF

JACK RUDLOE

The ocean has been good to me. With my nets, biological dredges, and diving gear I have made a delightful living by selling her wonderful renewable resources—the living creatures that dwell in her waters and live on her bottom. I have hauled out nets gorged with struggling fish, swum through coral reefs so breathtaking with their varieties of colors, strange-looking fish, and eerie monsters that the scenes have been etched forever in my memory. I have weathered storms at sea, lived with thundering waves pounding the beaches and howling winds during a hurricane, and taken advantage of her treasures cast upon the beach when the sea calms.

More than four decades have passed since I started Gulf Specimen Company, a small collecting enterprise. I settled in Panacea—a tiny fishing village in northwest Florida, so small that it seldom appears on maps—and began working with shrimpers, crab fishermen, and gill netters. As time passed, the demand for specimens from schools, research laboratories, and hobbyists increased, and with the demand I had to learn more about the behavior and ecology of the marine animals and plants of the Gulf of Mexico and the Atlantic Coast. There was, and still is, much to learn.

A collecting business is subject to tides, winds, and weather. It follows the movements of jellyfish, the migrations of squid, the ripeness of sea urchin eggs and the spawning patterns of polychaete worms. Large conchs spew out ribbons of accordion-like egg capsules, and purple sea hares ooze copious green strings containing millions of jelly-coated eggs. Female blue crabs carry thousands of developing larvae under their aprons in the form of a sponge, and commercial shrimp migrate to the deep waters of the Atlantic and the Gulf and explosively burst forth sperm and egg that unite— and the tiny planktonic larvae drift shoreward with the tides and currents, along with uncountable numbers of fish eggs, larval fish, and a host of other developing creatures. The ocean is so full of life, so productive that one can only marvel at it.

At midnight in the calm bays and estuaries of north Florida, you sometimes hear male porpoises letting out exuberant whimpering calls to their mates, and under the moonlight you hear them splashing about. Then the lumbering sea turtle comes ashore, dragging her heavy shell over the white sands and depositing her eggs high up on the beach.

Throughout the marshes and mangrove swamps shorebirds lay their eggs and the young hatch and feed upon the tiny fish and fiddler crabs. The waters become milky with veliger larvae of oysters during the spawning seasons, and soon the wharf pilings and dead shells are growing anew with tiny young oysters. The waters teem with gametes of sponges, tunicates, hydroids, and tiny crustacea, which unite and settle on the bottom.

The ocean does not give up easily the secrets of where to find these animals. Only by traveling around and diligently searching in her rock piles and mudflats, day after day and year after year, will you learn when creatures spawn and what they eat and where they hide. And that is what I have done, together with my wife Anne, for many years. Still, we know full well as we walk over our favorite salt marsh or fishing area, someone is probably looking at an aerial photograph of the same area, planning to dredge and fill it, or make it into a parking lot, shopping center, or housing development. I have come to hate those little red land-survey flags that suddenly appear in the marshes or in beautiful wooded forests; they are as characteristic of destruction as the chancre sore is of syphilis.

I long ago realized that I had to get involved. I could not close my eyes to evil and just go on collecting specimens and selling them to universities. If I did not take action, it was obvious that nothing would stop the destruction of north Florida estuaries. Our surveys have not stopped, but we have also engaged in a long-term campaign to educate the public through a barrage of lectures, field trips, television and radio interviews, and articles. I risk unpopularity by speaking out at every public forum that affects the land and waters I love.

Oil and gas drilling will surely degrade Florida's Gulf, perhaps more than any other source of pollution we have so far inflicted. All the ways we enjoy our coast—fishing, boating, shrimping, swimming—are at risk if we allow drilling proposals to go forward.

Jack Rudloe manages Gulf Specimen Marine Laboratories and has written nine books on the sea, including his latest, co-authored with his wife Anne, Shrimp: The Endless Quest for Pink Gold. He has long attested to the fact that shrimp and oil do not mix, especially tiny fragile larval shrimp.

ICHTHUS

O. VICTOR MILLER

Too drunk to sit in church, I kayak up the Wakulla River to sojourn with a spawning school of mullet.

Ichthus is Greek for this holiest of fishes. Before there was a church, lion-wary Christians scratched icon pictographs on aqueducts and inside caves among the ancient graffiti. To them, the mullet symbolized redemption from original naughtiness and lots of other stuff. For me, the mullet is a sort of sub-aquatic dove, a transcendental spirit. She jumps for the joy of mediating sky and sea and mud, the prototypal meat of everybody—a leap of faith ignoring gravity, trailing microcosmic beads of quicksilver.

The sacred spark that embers in all living things inspires the humble mullet's flight, the way I see it. She leaps toward Heaven to divine her destination relative to Earth, to see which way she's headed.

I think she jumps because she can't quite fly, though

she has seen it done by cormorants and ospreys splashing through the quasi-limits of a mirrored world to fly away with goat-eyed kin in beak or talon.

At night the mullet rockets through a floating moon, into a milky smudge of stars against the outer dark. She doesn't shake or turn in flight like tarpon do, but gives herself to toxic air, riding out the ecstasy of self-propelled momentum. She sails forever, flashing silver-plated mail right back to heaven. Then she splats back through refracted shadows of a perfect self, the soul of mullet, shucking off an incidental parasite or two.

She's fruitful, too, and quick to multiply. She spawns in daylight with the other fishes. At night her lunar image on the water fractures kaleidoscopically, cloning silver shards and slivers. She is a dewy water-lily spirit, who doesn't toil beyond a mild meander through the swaying grass. Nor does she spin, except the gold and silver threads her leaps of faith unravel from the floating yarn of sun and moon, and these her darting shuttle weaves into the sacred tapestry of life or slings a lasso round a bank of brooding clouds.

Most kosher of fishes, she has scales and swims in sweet accord with Deuteronomy. No unclean detritus passes through her osculating lips or grainy gizzard—no ort of tainted meat (nor any meat at all) except by accident. Thus it's known that seven of her kith were of the kind to sacrifice their unpolluted flesh to mobs that gathered on the pristine shores of Galilee.

For multitudes, a feast of mullet can be stretched out pretty thin with barley loaves or grits. There's also mullet soup and stew, or you can butterfly a mullet flat and nail her to a board to dry in smoke or sunshine. I like to make medallions with a cookie cutter and fry them crispy as a melting host upon the tongue. Oh man!

But *whoa!* Two shotgun blasts, one fast behind the other, shatter drowsy culinary musings. I jackknife up *in situ*—a startled Ishmael floating in a Queequeg's coffin—momentum squirts my kayak from the rushes. And lo, I see a fleecy-haired old fart some twice my age of sixty-seven. He's cruising up the channel herding fishes with his wooden prow. A mullet jumps. At the zenith of ascent she doesn't rise or fall, but pauses on insubstantial air, frozen into the eternity of now. The codger snatches up his heirloom gun and cocks both hammers, shouldering it. He fires both barrels, broadcasting stippled pewter across reflected sky and overhanging oak limbs toupeed in resurrection fern and whiskered in Spanish moss.

"What! Shooting mullet?" I exclaim.

He breaks his gun, reloading, eyes wild as brimstones, dead on me. "Oh God, I'm next," I think, though I'm no mullet. My fibrillating heart sends centrifugal waves against its ribbed thoracic hull. The kayak palsies, radiating chop.

"Been at it forty years," the geezer bleats, an old poot deaf from shooting. Then he aims those goddamn eyes upstream again to focus out about a thousand cubits. "I shoot the fuckers when they level off," he says, "just like a partridge on the covey rise. And then the bastard is a sitting duck."

"I'd never get a shot off quick enough," I say. "You ever kill any?"

"Not *yet*," he snarls. He sets his stubble chin upriver, cracks his throttle with apocalyptic vengeance. As if the time for bagging fish were near at hand, he leaves me wobbling in his smoking wake, confounded.

O. Victor Miller, a native Georgian, lives nomadically on areas of the planet that still support old growth and healthy living things. Clyde Edgerton calls Miller a cross between Harry Crews and Larry Brown. A novelist, humorist, and naturalist, he is a frequent contributor to Gray's Sporting Journal. *This piece is written in Miller's characteristic style, called "viction." More information found at http://www.ovictormiller.com/.*

VIEW FROM THE MOUND

DOUG ALDERSON

Compared to the surrounding landscape, Cedar Key's five-acre Shell Mound is a mountain. Its twenty-eight-foot summit affords a panoramic view of marshes, islands, and blue waters that has changed little since the time of the Timucua Indians, an early people who lived, loved, and ate along the Gulf for 2,500 years or more. The Timucua, generation after generation, built this mound from discarded oyster, clam, and whelk shells.

People still fish these waters and harvest shellfish. In fact, Cedar Key clam farming—begun as a retraining program for out-of-work fishermen after Florida's commercial net ban went into effect in 1995—is now a multi-million-dollar industry. Cedar Key bivalves continue to feed people as they did in ancient times.

The seagrass beds here along the Big Bend Coast are the most intact and expansive in the Gulf, providing homes for a multitude of commercially viable marine species. According to the Florida Fish and Wildlife Conservation Commission, a single acre can support an astounding forty thousand fish and 50 million invertebrates. Seagrass beds are among the most productive habitats on earth.

The rich marine life of the area has attracted birds through the eons. Wading birds, roseate spoonbills, and great flocks of ducks, ibis, and white pelicans frequent the waters. Ospreys and bald eagles soar across the skies. Mullet leap inexplicably, and dolphins drive fish against marshy shores for easy feeding.

In the past few years, sea kayakers on both short- and long-distance journeys are paddling these productive waters in greater numbers, helping to create a robust ecotourism economy. They are reminiscent of early dugout paddlers, except most seem more inclined to take away memories instead of fish.

All of this could change with oil drilling. Ironically, the island town of Cedar Key juts three miles into the Gulf, marking the boundary where oil drilling is being considered in state waters.

One spill in these shallow waters would suffocate seagrass and shellfish, coat birds with crude oil, and harm the region's biological productivity for generations. Furthermore, the rigs, pipelines, and support industries would likely change Cedar Key from an ecotourist haven to an industrial port, harkening back to the town's mid-1800s shipping heyday when bars, brothels, and gambling establishments lined its wharf, and one travel writer labeled it "the toughest town in the South." Most men carried one or two pistols and a bowie knife. This was Dodge City, Gulf Coast style.

Cedar Key has a history of boom and bust, whether it was importing and exporting goods, harvesting coastal cedar trees for pencils, or capturing sea turtles for food. Oil is no different. Drilling will further enable our oil addiction until we are forced, kicking and screaming, into the post-fossil-fuel age decades too late.

We are at a pivotal point in our history, much like the Timucua faced with the Spanish onslaught. The difference? Our arrows have to be words that pierce greed and illusion, opening hearts that have been hardened by false promises.

Currently, the Cedar Key Chamber of Commerce has a motto for the area's relaxed atmosphere: "where time stood still." Its public lands and absence of chain restaurants and motels hold promise that Cedar Key can become a "sustainable destination"—viable as a unique tourism magnet for generations to come.

Sitting atop the Timucua Shell Mound gives me perspective. Civilizations and towns have risen and fallen over millennia. People have peeled back the skin of Mother Earth to work the land and build their homes, only to have their works one day covered again by the wild green of life—or washed away by storms and the rising sea. Nothing remains of the Timucua villages except for this mound, towering above the surrounding marshlands like a beacon from the past.

What will we of the oil age leave behind for future generations in one hundred or one thousand years?

It is up to us to decide.

A winner of three national writing awards, Doug Alderson is the author of Waters Less Traveled: Exploring Florida's Big Bend Coast *and other works. His newest book,* Encounters with Florida's Endangered Wildlife, *is forthcoming from the University Press of Florida in 2010. To learn more, log onto http://www.dougalderson.net/.*

NORTH CAROLINA TRIUMPH

JAN DEBLIEU

On an afternoon in late spring the breakers that roll ashore on Cape Hatteras are a milky jade, a color that reminds me of how far south we are, and how close to the Gulf Stream. Just off the beach young gannets hunt, folding their wings as they dive smoothly into the sea. Behind them green water stretches to the horizon.

I am looking out at four thousand miles of wilderness. There is nothing between the beach where I stand and Africa.

It might have been very different. Twenty-five years ago the federal government and American oil companies envisioned a floating industrial city out there. There would have been drill ships and well heads and pipelines bringing natural gas and oil to an onshore processing facility. Now—so far—there is nothing but clean open water.

You often hear that our communities are too fragmented and powerless to fight social and environmental injustices, that people are too busy, too shortsighted, too selfish. You hear that democracy doesn't work anymore because politicians listen only to the lobbyists. I don't think that's always true. When enough people protest, over and over, it's possible to effect change. If you want to see the proof, come to the North Carolina Outer Banks and sail east.

Plans to drill off the Outer Banks quietly surfaced in 1981, when the federal government sold the mineral rights to a block of leases forty miles off Cape Hatteras. At the time the Outer Banks were still sparsely populated, and the lease sale did not attract much attention. Federal officials completed an initial environmental impact statement, which included little about the biology or physical dynamics of the lease blocks. Nothing more was done until 1988, when a consortium of companies led by Mobil Oil applied for permits to drill.

Sinking oil and gas wells offshore is a risky venture because of the danger of blowouts and pipeline ruptures, as well as the daily increments of pollution. Off Hatteras, conditions were what the oil companies called "challenging." The north-flowing Gulf Stream collides with a tendril of the southbound Labrador Current there, creating fast-moving knots and plumes that change daily, even hourly. More than two thousand feet below the surface the ocean bottom dips and rises and abruptly dips. The region is also beset by hurricanes.

Mobil and its partners hoped to find a large deposit of natural gas in an area of the Atlantic known locally as the Point. The deep waters there are home to rare sea turtles and birds, whales and dolphins, tuna, marlin, and sailfish. Floating mats of saffron-colored algae, holding tiny crabs and shrimp, drift west from the Sargasso Sea. Flying fish skip over the waves like emerald darts.

Would offshore drilling pose dangers to our communities and beautiful waters? A group of Outer Banks residents started doing research and talking to people from shores where drilling had already taken place. We didn't like what we found: tales of routine pollution, frequent small oil spills, and land washing away where canals had been dug for pipelines. Also, social problems like crime, prostitution, illegal gambling, and drugs all seemed to follow the sudden industrialization of coastal towns.

To our dismay, the county commissioners were inclined to listen to arguments that drilling would be good for the local economy. Why shouldn't we diversify? The rigs would be out of sight of land. They were unmoved by pictures of weed from the Sargasso Sea that had washed ashore, which showed that oil from the drill site could reach our beaches. The industrialization of our waters was to be undertaken for what seemed to us to be paltry gain—an estimated 5 trillion cubic feet of natural gas, less than what's needed to supply the nation's energy needs for three months.

Fortunes sometimes change in curious ways. In the winter of 1989 the opponents of offshore drilling felt as though we were invisible. Nobody seemed to be listening to us. But one evening that March, a tanker christened the *Exxon Valdez* wrecked on a shoal in Alaska's Prince William Sound. Eleven million gallons of oil spilled into one of the most pristine natural systems on Earth. By the next morning, the communities of the Outer Banks had closed ranks against the oil companies.

What followed was a beautiful exercise in democracy. Liberal environmentalists and conservative business owners worked together to convince state and federal authorities that the oil companies should not be granted the permits needed to drill. The people of the Outer Banks spoke with one voice—and our elected officials listened.

Our fight lasted twelve years. But in the autumn of 2000, the oil companies gave up all rights to the lease blocks they'd purchased off Cape Hatteras.

Today there are no active oil or gas leases off our shores. Even nine years later, writing that brings tears to my eyes.

In the current debate, Florida faces challenges similar to

what North Carolina confronted so long ago. You are being asked to sacrifice virgin wilderness for paltry gain—enough petrochemicals to lower the price of a gallon of gas a few pennies, if that. You are being asked to do this only months after a blown rig off northwest Australia pumped thousands of gallons of oil into the Timor Sea, in a modern reenactment of the *Exxon Valdez* disaster. You are being implored to allow drilling even as the United States fails to enact a national policy that stresses what will help us the most—aggressive energy conservation.

As often as I can, I visit the Cape Hatteras beaches and face east to whitecaps and scudding clouds. It's hard to place a monetary value on the beauty I see. But it's fair to say that the opponents to offshore drilling have ransomed it with our time, our sweat, our hearts. In summer dolphins frolic just past the breakers, and shorebirds play tag with the crystal waves. Fall and winter bring storms, yes, but also lines of sea ducks and an occasional spouting whale. Our waters are still clear and full of life, our air still unsullied. For now.

Jan DeBlieu is the author of four books about people and nature, most recently The Year of the Comets. *Her book* Wind *was awarded the 1999 John Burroughs Medal for Natural History Writing. She lives and writes on the North Carolina Outer Banks.*

THE WAY OF ALL FLESH

THOMAS HALLOCK

In late September, when the south Florida heat finally breaks, Sweetie and I head to the beach. We stay at mom-and-pop places on Treasure Island, off Saint Petersburg. The Sands. The Sea Chest. The Buccaneer Inn and Resort. Built in the mid-twentieth century from poured concrete, these old motor lodges offer few amenities besides a pool, shuffleboard court, kitchenette, a grill for cook outs, and, of course, the Gulf. Rates are reasonable; people come from around the world to stay here, often for weeks at a time.

Sadly the vintage motels have not aged well. Salt air is corroding the steel in their concrete walls, causing the buildings to rot from inside. The owners, faced with increased property values, sell rather than repair. And the developers favor tall condos, which are empty most of the year. Now, instead of two-story motels tucked behind the dunes, there are rows of shuttered windows along the beach. This is how things go in Florida: what is funky, beautiful, or cool gets taken away.

Sweetie and I enjoy the camp on Treasure Island while we still can.

We pack a cooler with peeled shrimp, a bag of Doritos, and a six of Red Stripe. Twenty bucks gets us a cabana for the day. We spread our towels over the wood loungers and wait for the same girl who is there every year to collect the fee. She drives from cabana to cabana in a heaving pick-up. She is tan, twenty-something, tattooed, and wears a bikini top and denim cut-offs with the top button open. She took over the job, she explains, from her dad. Before this, she waited tables at The Wing House, a local chain of sports bars that features boobies, beer, and fatty meat. "There was no one there to have an intelligent conversation with," she complained.

On a Friday afternoon, Sweetie and I share the beach with a few other tourists. The mood is mellow. Coral-beaked terns congregate at the surf's edge; with their heavy black crests, they look like a flock of Elvis impersonators. Leather-skinned old ladies stroll along the shore line. Kids tote plastic buckets to a rising castle. A cheap umbrella blows across the sand. A plane circles overhead, the banner tow—"Eat at Gators"—tugs against the sky. Sweetie and I read, nap, snack, read some more.

After a few hours we go for a swim, shuffling deeper and deeper into the warm, green, amniotic Gulf. Fish peck at our feet. Dolphins pop above the surface and disappear again. The construction on a new condo rattles behind us. Cumulus clouds gather against the blue sky, promising a late afternoon storm. I turn my back to the noise. Sweetie wraps her arms around my upper back and her legs around my waist. We rise and fall with the swelling Gulf. She gives me a kiss. I look over her shoulder. There is nothing but open sea.

Thomas Hallock is an Assistant Professor of English at the University of South Florida Saint Petersburg. He is the author and editor of several academic books, including the forthcoming William Bartram, the Search for Nature's Design: Selected Letters, Art, and Unpublished Writings, *to be released in 2010 by University of Georgia Press.*

STORMY BEACH

JEFF KLINKENBERG

I like to go to the beach in a storm. I like to go to the beach nearest to my home in Saint Petersburg when lightning bolts are crashing down like pitchforks thrown by Zeus from Mount Olympus. I like fighting the wind to open the door to my truck and feeling the sting of sand against my skin. Finally, I like the solitude of the beach, the utter loneliness of the beach. If you live in crowded coastal Florida, it is the only time you have the beach, and the wilderness the beach represents, to yourself.

Boom! That was close. I stay in my truck, windshield wipers keeping time with my beating heart. Australian pines, bobbing and weaving in the squall, evade no punches. Laughing gulls know enough to hunker in the dunes.

Most summers the weather is inconvenient for the sun worshipers among us, but perfect for those of us who have no use for the beach in the traditional manner. My years of sitting on a towel and basting for hours are behind me. I hate the hustle and bustle of finding a parking place, putting money in a meter and listening to loud music or intrusive conversation. Plus, I am tired of hearing my dermatologist cluck with disapproval as she whittles away strategic patches of a forehead once thought handsome.

As a beach consumer, I am looking for open spaces and room to think. Such beaches exist in the Florida Panhandle. A few months ago, as I hiked such a beach near Apalachicola on an overcast day, a family of deer traipsed across a vast sand dune. Where I live in west-central Florida, I don't count on seeing deer. But if I want the beach to myself, I go in the rain. Better yet, I wait for a storm.

Clogs of dead sea oats fly down the beach like tumbleweed. I wear glasses to protect my eyes against the blasts of sand. The rain beats down so hard the surf seems bruised and bleeding. But rain is rain and sea is sea; if the surf were King Kong, it would be beating its chest in triumph. As a teenager, I loved to surf in heavy weather. As a middle-aged adult, mortality no longer an abstract, I am less inclined to get my feet wet. I know if I tried to wade out in this surf, I'd be swept to my doom.

For some of us, perhaps that is the appeal of the beach in a storm. It's a wild place, a dangerous place, utterly indifferent to humanity. "The sea speaks a language polite people never repeat," wrote Carl Sandburg. Man, it can knock you for a loop.

In interior Florida, the great predators—Florida panthers and black bears and Eastern diamondback rattlesnakes—are quickly vanishing as forests are laid bare. Dip your toe into the surf at even an urban beach and you've entered a wilderness ruled by sharks that will eat you if they are hungry enough. "The sea—this truth must be confessed—has no generosity," wrote Joseph Conrad.

The squall passes, the lightning calls a truce. In the lull I walk the deserted beach toward the jetty. When a flock of black skimmers whips by, I am the audience. Farther offshore a pair of dolphins reveal their dorsal fins. Closer in, a school of cownose rays flaps majestically past.

A pitiful sailor, I can get seasick staring at a glass of water. I prefer *terra firma*. Watching a roiled sea from the beach on a stormy day is like having a ringside seat at a prizefight. The excitement is not necessarily accompanied by a bloody nose. I take a moment to sit in the sand and read my worn copy of *The Sea and the Jungle*, H.M. Tomlinson's account of a voyage across the Atlantic to the Amazon in a tramp steamer in 1909. "I had never seen so much lively water so close," he wrote of his trip aboard the *Capella*. "She wallowed, she plunged, she rolled, she sank heavily to its level."

Fighting *mal de mer*, and also concerned about the arrival of the latest squall, I retire to my pickup truck. Here comes the rain. Here comes a wind even more powerful than the wind before. As my truck rocks, I pretend I'm on the crew of the *Capella* or, even better, I am standing on the deck of the *Pequod*, with my harpoon-toting friend Queequeg, waiting for Ahab to issue the order to lower the boats. Call me Ishmael.

Jeff Klinkenberg is the Florida culture writer for the St. Petersburg Times. *His latest book collection of essays is* Pilgrim in the Land of Alligators. *Another anthology,* Seasons of Real Florida, *is also in print. His website is* http://www.jeffklinkenberg.com/.

NEARSHORE

JULIE MORRIS

For forty years, I have lived and worked within walking distance of Sarasota Bay. From my third floor office, I can see the wilderness to the west. When I first stood on this bayfront in 1970, not a single building broke the tree canopy on Longboat Key. Now I mark the seasonal swing from solstice to solstice by sunsets behind various condo towers. But Longboat Key is a sliver dwarfed by a vast sea of wildlife. Every week, I watch anglers with special gear and fast boats cast for red drum and spotted sea trout. I've seen herds of mating manatees drift by in summer. Each winter day, ospreys lift fish from the bay and settle in bayfront pines to eat. These experiences bind me to the bay and the Gulf. On my wild western horizon, the sunset sky is painted an edgy fluorescence in the winter, softly pastel in the summer. When crepuscular rays fade to twilight, the evening star draws my eye.

Last October, I flew from Tampa to Corpus Christi and peered down from the plane at the fragmented marshes of the Mississippi Delta. The oil platforms looked small from 35,000 feet, but the pipelines and boat canals connecting nearshore oil to the mainland have hugely scarred and degraded the delta marshes. Louisiana anglers tell me that fishing is great around the rigs, and new techniques for laying pipeline are sleek and swift. But I also hear that oil and gas interests in Louisiana use their political muscle to swiftly undermine any fish and wildlife conservation measures standing in the way of exploration and production.

The windy Corpus Christi landing strip runs along tank farms and refineries for Citgo and Valero gasoline. Smoke stack flares, complicated pipework, and heavy industrial air make for a special Texas welcome. In downtown Corpus, the wide bay beach looks east to barrier islands and the open Gulf beyond. But this is no wilderness view. A tank farm, refinery, and shipyard at Ingleside throb with orange industrial light all night. At dusk my eye is drawn there, not to the glowing planets in the darkening sky.

My tentative ventures into Florida's nearshore waters are the reverse of a sea turtle on the beach. On early summer nights, female loggerheads haul out on dark beaches to dig sandy nests and drop their eggs. For sea turtles, dry land is a foreign, anxious place to be. Once their nests are laid and properly disguised, loggerheads return to the water with speed and focus. Their normal, comfortable habitats are the broad live bottoms and grass beds stretching west and south along Florida's Gulf Coast where they drift and dive all year.

In contrast, I am a land creature making short forays into salt water. I rarely swim at the beach beyond where I can stand. I have paddled both an aluminum canoe and a plastic kayak more than a mile from shore, one time parallel to the marshes of Saint Marks and another time along the headlands of Naples. On a friend's boat, I caught my limit of red snapper and vermilion in eighty feet of water south of Pensacola. I have surface dived to gather scallops in lush turtle grass beds off Steinhatchee.

I ask friends from Venice, Louisiana, how far from shore the rigs need to be to drop from view beyond the horizon.

"Fifteen miles," they say. "But," one friend adds, "no one wants to see rigs from the beach when they vacation in Destin. People accept the industrialized coast of Louisiana and Texas, but they expect something different and better in Florida."

Like millions of Floridians, I encounter the wildness of Gulf nearshore waters in deep and meaningful ways. This attachment to wildness and beauty is part of our shared Florida identity, and it motivates us to work for civic good and a better future. Sully this motivating attachment and become more like Texas and Louisiana? No way.

Julie Morris lives in Sarasota and works at New College, Florida's public honors college. For three decades and half of her life, she's explored the Gulf's shallow edges and deliberated Gulf conservation policies—in the 1980s as a Sierra Club leader, in the 1990s as a Florida Fish and Wildlife Commissioner, and since 2001 on the Gulf of Mexico Fishery Management Council.

WHAT FLORIDA THEN?

JONO MILLER

I don't know if my grandfather's grandfather ever got south of Kissimmee. He pioneered a citrus grove on an island in Lake Harris north of Okahumpka. I struggle to imagine what Florida was like then, with alligators walking down the sand streets.

When he wasn't at Lake Harris, my great-great-grandfather, one of the trustees of the Internal Improvement Fund, was in Tallahassee. When the trustees authorized the sale of 4 million acres of one of the planet's most distinctive wetland systems for 25 cents an acre (about $5.30 an acre today), my ancestor probably had never seen nor appreciated the Everglades.

We'll never know to what extent those trustees were motivated by perceived fiscal desperation on behalf of the state and to what extent theirs was an infectious exuberance brought on by the possibilities of a new economic engine. We do know that from the earliest grants to railroads, to the sale of the Everglades, to the sale of submerged-land leases to facilitate dredge and fill projects (3.6 million acres leased for around a penny an acre), that the State of Florida frequently has seemed far too willing to divest citizens of the state's natural resources when leaders perceived a buck was to be made. We seem to have a flair for selling Florida on the cheap.

Florida has been blessed with remarkably diverse habitats, many of which occur nowhere else. It is gratifying to realize how much the state has done right, how we lead in protecting our remaining natural areas, and how we have set aside many of the state's rarest and most popular habitats for the public's use and enjoyment.

Of all the dozens of habitats there is only one, just one single place, where people are not only entitled to visit but feel so at home that they routinely take off most of their clothes and lie down. They dare carcinomas to be there.

There really are no beaches in the world like the sugar-sand beaches of the Gulf of Mexico. Clearwater Beach, Destin, Siesta Key, Panama City, Pensacola Beach—each of them vies to have their beach called the most dazzling and coolest in the nation.

This past June, Dennis Arentz of Reading, Pennsylvania, wrote to the *Sarasota Herald-Tribune* not to complain about hotel prices, nor to rant about traffic or surly service. He wrote as a tourist Paul Revere to alert Sarasotans that their county was "dumping regular gray sand" on Siesta Beach. Dingy gray sand doesn't turn white. The last line of his plea? "It would be a shame to lose tourism dollars by ruining a beautiful, unique beach like Siesta Key."

The selling of Florida's natural inheritance is a ratchet wheel that turns in but one direction. Promises of profit and salvation yield to seller's remorse and fading memories. We struggle to understand what was squandered. My mind wants to query my grandfather's grandfather, yet my heart turns to my granddaughter's granddaughter. What Florida then?

Jono Miller is a natural historian and environmentalist who works at New College of Florida and is currently pursuing a master's degree in the Florida Studies Program at University of South Florida in Saint Petersburg. He believes in Florida, cabbage palms, chickens, the Myakka, water demand management, trees, canoeing, and gardens.

THE GULF OF MEXICO

GRACE C. JACKSON

The Gulf of Mexico would be empty without its creatures great and small

Its clear and clean waves crashing, splashing, foaming as they fall

Without its bright darting fish swimming driftily

Without its crying seabirds swirling free

Without its scuttling crabs running across the sand

Without its schooling minnows darting near the land

Without its brightly-colored shells speckling the shore.

Florida's Gulf would be empty if these wonders existed there no more

Without its fun-filled dolphins leaping with joy.

We should all treat our Gulf like a respected friend not a toy.

It would be empty without its osprey
rising from the water gracefully with pride

Without its tiny creatures floating at the mercy of the tide

Without its manatees drifting slowly through a bay

Without its little hermit crabs scuttling in play

Without its horseshoe crab crawling along the sand

Without its nurse shark cruising as if his route is planned.

All of these animals call the Gulf of Mexico home

Where they reproduce, live, eat and die and this place is where

they should always have the right to freely roam.

Grace C. Jackson is a third grader who loves to draw, write, run down the beach, and go everywhere barefoot. She lives in Tallahassee with her mom, dad, and older brother Zachary, along with their greyhound, parakeet, leopard gecko, and two enormous goldfish.

PATIENCE AT THE PASS

EDWARD C. WOODWARD

In our frenetic era, we have no patience for progress. We need tweets and slogans and texts with one letter or number words—no time 4 vowels. Wanting a break from that pace, and perspective to write about why we need to keep Florida's ban on offshore drilling, I'm taking my six-year-old daughter, Anna, to Stump Pass Beach State Park on the Gulf of Mexico.

But switching my senses from a frenetic pace to a beach pace takes time, such as standing still and silent on the sand watching plump brown pelicans gracefully defy gravity. So until we reach Stump Pass in Englewood, my mind races for quick solutions—or slogans—as Interstate fast food exit signs whir by: "Chick Filet. Closed Sunday." Hey, how about "Florida Gulf Coast Drilling. Closed Every Day."

Why Stump Pass? So I can see an evolving beach nourishment project my AmeriCorps service team planted six years ago, when my daughter was a baby. Have the sea grapes, sea oats, and railroad vines, given time, crawled from infancy to nurture the beach? I think of cultivating alternative energy sources the same way: give them time to grow. Seeing the Stump Pass project will remind me, as well as show my daughter the benefits of long-term planning and patience.

At Stump Pass, Anna finds a bamboo stick and traces our names in the soft sand, then scampers to the shoreline like the sanderlings that live on the beach. Nearby a couple plucks seashells from a crumbling sand wall, two men cast lines for grouper and redfish, and three young women, laughing and linked like paper dolls, steady each other in the swirling waves stirred by Tropical Storm Ida. It's November and most beachgoers are wearing short sleeves and shorts. Floridians and shorebirds flock to the beach year-round because we can.

Meanwhile, Anna skitters barefoot through the surf, shrieking, squealing, and laughing wildly as only an uninhibited six-year-old can, sandy, salty, and happy. "Brrrrr," she says. "This is fun!" This is Florida ice skating— feet gliding, graceful play. The moment spawns another idea for an anti-drilling slogan: a prohibition sign over an oil rig with the words, "I *Break* for Surf Skating. So Don't spOIL the fun." Banning drilling is the only surefire way to avoid a drilling accident.

Soon Anna and I build sandcastles bridged together. But a frothy wave annexes our castles. We need a moat. So with shells as shovels, we carve a protective barrier. Another wave. "Ahhhhh!" Anna yelps. The castles are flattened, and the moat floods. "We can wait," she says. "Wait for what?" I ask. "For the moat to get bigger." Patience. We keep digging.

Before leaving Stump Pass, I show Anna the site of my AmeriCorps beach project. Six years ago it was a sand canvas. Now clumps of sea oats and railroad vine tentacles hug the ground. Sea grape trees from gallon plants now stand as six foot sentries buffering the beach. Six years is micro-tweet time on a planet billions of years old. Patience.

I understand and appreciate the benefits of oil and gas. My wife and I need oil to take our two children to parks so they can experience conservation. Invaluable organizations benefitting people and animals need oil, for now. Our AmeriCorps team needed oil to park-hop by van throughout central and southwest Florida so we could remove invasive exotic plants that choke out native species. Slogan idea: "Drilling Gone Wild: An Exotic Florida's Beaches Can *Live* Without."

But other sources for oil and gas exist. Hopefully, if patient, we can wait on alternative energy sources to take root. Florida can't afford to risk its internationally revered natural resources. Not just for the tourist industry, but for creatures seen and unseen. Consider the words of naturalist John Muir, "The universe would be incomplete without man, but it would also be incomplete without the smallest transmicroscopic creature that dwells beyond our conceitful eyes and knowledge."

More than 140 years ago, Muir walked from Indiana to Cedar Key. He saw "the Gulf of Mexico stretching away unbounded, except by the sky. What dreams and speculative matter for thought arose as I stood on the strand, gazing out on the burnished, treeless plain."

Let's keep it that way, folks trekking from Indiana to see our beaches.

Edward C. Woodward is editor and co-founder of http:// www.paddleandpath.com/, a website about exploring Florida's woods and waterways. He has a master's degree in Florida Studies from the University of South Florida, Saint Petersburg.

THE SOUL OF THE GULF

LINDA TAYLOR

I do not have many clear memories of my childhood. But the one that is most vivid is of a day in September when my friend and I hauled oil-soaked ducks in our wagons from the beach in southern New Jersey to her mother's laundry room. I had not heard my parents talk of an oil spill nor was there any environmental organization instructing citizens on what to do to save these poor creatures. It was just my friend and I trying to figure out why we could not get this oil off the feathers with laundry detergent. As the day drew on and we grew more and more sticky with this dark coating of death, we were tasked with towing the birds back to the beach for their sad burial in the sand.

For most of the year, the waters of the Gulf of Mexico embrace the western shoreline of Florida with a calm hand. We are cupped in her protective palm until the inevitable hurricane passes into the Gulf, reminding us of the power this body of water has over the borrowed land we call home. The hurricane by whatever its name—Charlie, Wilma, Katrina—is a reminder that we cannot control or dominate nature, that we must listen, for nature always has something to say. We cannot manipulate or destroy in the name of dollars. The Gulf has a spirit that is linked to our own. Science cannot shout down justice. Policy will not replace health. Economics is not spirituality.

I have not read any concrete evidence that drilling in the Gulf of Mexico for oil will improve our lives. With such a large number of hard-working individuals searching to better their quality of life, the probing and drilling of such an incredible body of water will only add to the helplessness of despair. We know that drilling for oil off the coast of Florida will put our sea turtles, whales, fisheries, shorebirds, and local economies at serious risk. Just as importantly, drilling would impact our sense of place. At a time when humanity is searching for hope, we need the magnificence of our natural wonders. Looking out at the sea—the Gulf of Mexico—with only clouds, a sunset, or the silhouette of a sailboat to interrupt the horizon, we see endless possibilities. With thousands of visitors sharing this experience with residents, the Gulf touches so many every day.

We calculate risks and benefits with statistics from research. But can we analyze the human spirit and how our constant quest to probe nature for economic wealth affects our mental and spiritual health?

Each time we scar nature, we scar our own souls. With every violation of an ecosystem, we see the impact heading towards our own well-being. Our health is directly linked to the health of this earth and the waters that balance the elements. We cannot probe, drill, or dig without consequences. If the oil companies try to harness the energy in the Gulf of Mexico, we will see a negative impact on the energy surrounding these waters.

My body and spirit were born from the sea. Through osmosis my cells contain salt water. I am able to feel the ocean's turbulence when it is roiling and its peace when it is still. I know that I must live close to this life-giving element of my being. I also must speak for what gives me life, for the waters of the Gulf of Mexico are vibrating with the terror of the possibility of this violent penetration—she would much prefer to float platforms of wind turbines.

The time has come to consider spirituality alongside science, and to consider that healthy economics means a healthy natural world and that the actions of the community are linked to our spirit. Do not drill into our soul.

Linda Taylor has lived on Clearwater Beach for twenty years. She is the author of Great Women Exploring Nature: How Wild Florida Influenced Their Lives. *She owns the fourteen-year-old company, It's Our Nature®, which features Healthy-Wear for People Who Care®, found at http://www.itsournature.com/.*

HEAD ABOVE WATER

MEGAN M. MELVIN

It can, has, and will make me cry. It is so often the
source of my daydreams, nightmares, and every emotion in
between. As a barrier island, it is small and fragile, yet has
been around for ages. It is constantly changing—eroding,
wearing down, building up—sometimes very rapidly, and
other times at a deceptively slow pace. But the going-away of
North Captiva Island has been hanging around like a cloud
of gnats ever since it has been a part of my life, which is silly
to say, I suppose, because there has never been a time when
it has not been a part of my life. Before me, and since me, it
has formed a considerable portion of the very fabric of my
family and of my existence on this Earth. For me, it's always
been there.

This island represents not only the closest approximation
of unspoiled beauty I have the privilege of knowing
intimately, it represents the foundation of every value
and institution I hold dear. Family. Loyalty. Laughter.
Respect. Peace. Triumph. Gratitude. Sharing. Good food and

drink. Simplicity. Life—living it and escaping from it. My grandparents discovered the island by accident, but now all of us—all fifty or so of us—feel as if the island belongs to us and we belong there.

We gather there to fish from the splintered old dock, to walk and collect, run and paddle and sleep. We lie in the sun and we cook simple, abundant, creative meals featuring the catch of the day. At night we linger around the dinner table to talk and play Scattergories and Scrabble. Sometimes we plan entertainment but the stars interrupt, or the phosphorescent shrimp run with the tide past the old pilings, or there may be a shark to glimpse down in the black water. There are birds and snakes, but most of the big animals—boar and panther—have been gone since before I was born. Things seem to be the same as they have always been, and we cling desperately to that notion, but we all quietly know that they are not.

My earliest memory takes place on North Captiva. My grandparents' house is situated on the lee side of the island around the corner from a wide, deep pass that is world-renowned for tarpon fishing. When I was three, I was playing in the crushed shells on the beach while my dad was cleaning fish on the dock. It was late afternoon, and that meant the tide was coming in hot. I was instructed not, under any circumstances, to enter the water. I was about fifty feet down the beach from the dock where my dad was working with his back to me, crawling in the sand and digging up coquina, when I spotted a brilliant orange giant starfish in about two feet of water. The contrast of cool crystal blue and vibrant fiery orange was too much for me—I waded into the water toward it, hand outstretched. My feet were promptly swept out from under me by an invisible riptide and I began tumbling, out of control, head half underwater, toward the barnacle-crusted pilings of the dock. At three I was already a fine swimmer, but there was no way in hell my little body carried enough weight to pull me out of the riptide. On the upward swing of a tumble, my head popped out of the water just long enough for me to yell "Daaa—!!"

He dove from the dock and grabbed me, maneuvering my body in front of his so that he was between me and the piling when the riptide pinned us against the razor-sharp, crusty wood. He could barely touch the bottom, but it was just enough, and he was on his way up the beach in a flash of water spray, carrying me by one arm. While I dangled from his iron grip, he used his free arm to spank me. I cried and protested until I saw the blood running down his back.

I don't ever want to feel that way again. I don't ever want to risk hurting something I love because of my recklessness and greed, my disregard, my desire to touch and grab and take.

My father's memories of the island are not that different from my own, or from his father's. The first time he saw it he recalls feeling like a member of Swiss Family Robinson—it was primitive, wild, a little scary—the adventure he'd been staging for years with his brothers in the Midwestern woods. He relished the opportunity to recreate this for the next generation of my cousins and me, spending hours drawing elaborate maps and leading us to all of the hidden treasures he'd spent his adolescence discovering.

It has been a learning experience for everyone, and sometimes we just get lucky. Once, my grandmother thought it would be nice to have some shark meat, so my grandfather went out at night to get a blacktip or nurse shark. He used a 14-foot pole with a five-prong spear attached to the end and connected the spear to his wrist with rope. When he speared a six-foot shark in the head, it began flipping madly in the shallow water, causing the spear to crack my grandfather directly in the eye and knock him off of the pier, and when the shark began swimming out to sea, he was still attached by the wrist. My grandparents picked my father up at the airport the next day, and my dad recalls the wrist looking like it had been stuck into a garbage disposal. "Betsy wanted shark," was his only explanation. "Won't do that again."

Before it was inhabited, Spanish pirates used to store beautiful women that they captured and enslaved on the island, hence the name Captiva. I wonder if my family, by planting ourselves there, by acting as the ultimate invasive species, is really any different. What we have captured is not as tangible and singular as a native slave, but it is just as beautiful and fragile and we guard it just as fiercely. We have managed to forge the essence of our strength, our connectedness, our love, onto this pile of sand and coral, and we use the landscape to hold these things captive. If we lose sight of them, all we need to do is get there. On the island, family ties are as physical as the vines that twist through the trees or a hook in the mouth of a red snapper.

I know that North Captiva will be gone someday. Someday soon even. The longer it does remain, the more it will change and the less I will recognize it. In my lifetime, I will return countless times, and on some of those visits, I will be unable to find familiar landmarks, features, and friends. My favorite gumbo-limbo trees will disappear. Already, what seemed the stuff of magic and mystery to a child looks smaller to an adult, somehow made plain. Whether due to the loss of the thick green roof of leaves and the panthers or something less specific, the island seems to be less of an enclosed Eden and more vulnerable and bare. It is difficult to experience refuge and exposure at the same time.

My father has saved my life on the island not once, but twice. One late night when I was seven, a group of us were on the dock trying to catch a shark. We had a different strategy this time—we had been saving fish carcasses for a few days and had strung them onto a massive, rusty hook, which we tied to a sturdy line, looped around a piling, and threw out towards the pass. The dock lights illuminated small circles of water, and outside of that there was nothing but salty breeze and muffled riffles that may or may not have been shark fins breaking the surface.

My five-year-old brother and I were wearing matching sweatpants and sweatshirts perfect for the cool Gulf breeze blowing in from the pass. We were both straining to see beyond the edge of the dock and the circles of light, out into the darkness. There was a yank on the line, a quick churn of the water below us, and my brother, in his eagerness to get closer to the action, ran up behind me and forgot to stop. His little-boy-clumsy crash into my back knocked me right off the side of the dock into the black water, way too close to the line, hook, and mysterious splashing. My thick cotton sweatsuit made swimming impossible, but before I even started to sink my dad's arm was around my chest, pulling me away from the blackness of the night and towards shore.

Megan M. Melvin is working toward her master's degree in literature at the University of Montana, where she also teaches composition. She enjoys dividing her time between the mountains of the West and the islands of the Gulf.

I DREAMED OF FLORIDA
MARTY AMBROSE

The state with the prettiest name,
the state that floats in brackish water,
held together by mangrove roots
that bear while living oysters in clusters
—ELIZABETH BISHOP, "FLORIDA"

When I first read this poem, I was in high school and ready to take my first trip to Florida to visit my uncle in Miami. I was stunned by Bishop's images of the "long S-shaped birds" and "enormous turtles, helpless and mild," and I anticipated tropical scenery very different from what I had grown up with in St. Louis.

I wasn't disappointed.

As my parents and I drove south on U.S. 1, I scanned the shoreline of the Atlantic Ocean along the Florida coast, endlessly fascinated by the orange and gold sunrises, the gracefully arching palm trees, the rolling tides, and the parade of oddly long-limbed birds. Breathtaking. Panoramic. Stirring.

During the visit, I had my first experience snorkeling at Pennekamp Coral Reef. My heart pounded with excitement as we headed out from Gilbert's Marina at dawn in a strong offshore breeze. The boat rocked as I slid into the cool water like a Weeki Wachee mermaid. I floated on the surface, my breath strong and steady, and I surveyed the explosion of color from the fish that hovered around the coral.

I never wanted to leave.

But I had to go home at the end of this vacation—only to return years later when my parents decided to move to Fort Myers and I had the chance to visit them.

Then, I saw my first southwest Florida beach. Mind you, that was over twenty-five years ago when Fort Myers Beach still had a swing bridge, sand dunes, and very little traffic. The island was quiet and quaint—and the water a sight to behold.

The Gulf of Mexico.

Water a soft blue, almost aquamarine, and sand a dazzling white, almost too bright to look at in the blinding summer sun.

I would spend almost the entire day floating on a raft in the warm water, staring up at the sun, enjoying the feel of the heat and salt on my skin. Fish swam around me and pelicans circled overhead as I daydreamed about a time when I could live in Florida year-round.

And it happened.

I now live on Pine Island full time, teach, and write mysteries. And at every opportunity, I canoe, swim, and snorkel in the Gulf, and I never tire of living on the coast.

Florida is truly a state of mind. A tropical dream. A place to live where I can be connected to nature through every outdoor activity.

Like Elizabeth Bishop, who lived in Key West during the Hemingway years, I don't want to see Florida become "the poorest postcard of itself" by not protecting its natural habitat. We can only do that by not forgetting that we are responsible for our environment and for the next generation ready to take that first trip to Florida.

And never want to leave.

Professor Marty Ambrose has worked at Edison State College for over two decades as a professor of English, communications chair, and now as assessment chair. In her spare time, she writes and publishes The Mango Bay Mystery Series with Avalon Press.

SANIBEL ISLAND

JESSE MILLNER

I kayaked out from a little spit in Ding Darling through corridors of mangrove, and then out to a small island in the middle of the bay. It was near dusk and the big condo towers on the edge of the water were filling with artificial light even as the low sun burned its clear promise of paradise coming before nightfall. I struggled against the wind to that green place amid the dark blue where frigatebirds sailed above, coal black bodies, split tails, and I thought of a friend's story about frigatebirds caught in the surprise of Hurricane Charlie, how they tried to stay together in 160-mph winds, how they followed each solitary stray, fought the storm to bring the lost one home, if indeed, home is where the beating wings are gathered, that heaven of shared dreams.

Pelicans everywhere and ibis, too. Herons and egrets, crows who wheel and caw above the island that looks as though it should sink from the weight of so many birds, but how light these creatures are, all feather and hollow bone, brains filled with rumors of fish blood and memories of tasty innards that spill their inky contents to the command of sharp beaks.

I float on the leeward side and stare at this multitude gathered in God's name, these true angels that live amongst us every minute, that define our lives as earthbound and futile. Confined by gravity, we are never able to surrender to that night sky, where the stars come on, and the stars come on, until there's a wilderness that glows.

The wind is behind me as I paddle back to the spit, black water catching the lights of passing cars on the causeway, burning muscles from the pull and draw as I dip my paddle into the infinite blue, and I imagine the Gulf stretching beyond this barrier island filled with salt winds and gulls, a world complete with motion and feathers, where angels rise and angels fall, depending on gravity and fish.

Jesse Millner's most recent book of poems is The Neighborhoods of My Past Sorrow. *He teaches writing courses at Florida Gulf Coast University and lives in Fort Myers with his wife, Lyn, and dog, Sam.*

BEWARE THE SIRENS
OF BIG OIL

RIKI OTT

In the early 1970s, Big Oil wooed Alaskans with a seductive chorus promising jobs, riches, and risk-free oil development, pipeline transfer, and tanker transport. Alaska politicians fell under its spell.

Today Big Oil generates more than 85 percent of Alaska's operating revenues—and the song has changed. The tune is now militant and strident, as the industry demands ever more opportunity to drill and ever less regulation. This "opportunity" comes at the expense of deeply rooted indigenous cultures, family lifestyles, and businesses like commercial fishing and tourism that rely on Alaska's abundant natural resources.

But the same enchanting siren music once tailored to Alaskans is currently playing for Floridians, Californians, and others who live on our seacoasts. From my perspective as a survivor of North America's largest oil spill—from the *Exxon Valdez* in 1989—it seems too many politicians are falling under its spell. My advice to coastal residents in the Lower 48: Take heed.

We learned the hard way that Big Oil's promises were good only until authorizing laws were passed and permits approved. The industry promised, for instance, in the early 1970s to double hull its tankers to minimize the risk of spills. But it will take until 2015—more than 40 years—for it to make good on this promise. That's too late for those of us in Prince William Sound. Ironically, too, 2015 will arrive long before the last of the toxic oil that spilled from the single-hulled *Exxon Valdez* is gone from our beaches—and long before our herring even begin to recover.

The once thriving multi-million-dollar herring fisheries are nonexistent and the wildlife that feed on herring—well, it will recover whenever the herring recover. Maybe. Scientists make no promises.

Safer tankers are no excuse to drill as the ongoing oil rig blowout in Australia illustrates. Oil will spill as long as oil is drilled because we are human, and humans err. The industry has yet to make good on another decades-old promise made when the tanker Torrey Canyon wrecked on Britain's shore in 1967. The industry still can't clean up oil when it washes ashore. "Nothing's changed," observed a retired oil port official in Shetland (Scotland) when I was there earlier this month.

The oil industry can certainly put on a good show of busy-ness for appearance's sake. Exxon spent billions during its 1989 cleanup—spill survivors call it a cover up—which was a tax write-off as a cost of doing business. The oil industry had promised residents that harsh dispersants (chemical products) would not be used on biologically sensitive beaches. Further, Exxon promised cleanup workers that its products were not toxic: "Just wear the right gear," they said. Dispersants and products with solvents were used on beaches. Adequate gear was not provided and thousands of workers became sick.

Exxon claimed the illnesses were colds and flu—the "Valdez Crud"—and the company fought workers who sued them for chemical poisoning. This saga is still playing out as Barnett and Lerner, an admiralty law firm in Florida, is taking ExxonMobil to court to pay for disabilities, medicine, health care, and lost wages of those who survived the failed 1989 cleanup.

Meanwhile, academics have reported that cleanup workers from tanker spills in Spain (2002) and South Korea (2007) were found to have respiratory damage, central nervous system damage, and even DNA (chromosome) damage from inhalation of oily mists and particulates—all hallmark symptoms of overexposure to oil. This leaves little doubt that *Exxon Valdez* cleanup workers suffered a similar fate, whether or not Exxon chooses to admit and take responsibility for their suffering.

Finally, Exxon promised to make the community whole after the spill. We naively took Exxon's word, not realizing that Exxon meant to the minimum extent mandated by law. The corporation, wielding ill-gained human rights and its enormous wealth, fought spill victims—common people—in court for over twenty years to minimize its liability and reduce the number of claims against them. Owners of tourism businesses and shoreside vendors that supported the commercial fishing industry were some of the first to have their claims thrown out of court despite serious losses. The bitterness and length of the lawsuit itself generated its own trauma that played out as decades of community dysfunction. In the end, people whose claims survived the twenty-year battle recovered about ten percent of their economic losses—and not one cent of the losses to culture or quality of life.

People in Florida, California, and other coastal states considering offshore oil should beware. What good will come of sabotaging your existing tourism and sport-fishing industries, and your beautiful coastlines where residents and visitors recreate, with the false promises of Big Oil? Our legal system will treat you no better than it did us in Alaska should your beaches become oiled.

Falling for the siren song will only indenture your state to an oil-dependent future that is already past. It's time to grow new green industries, rooted in regional strengths, rather than support transnational oil corporations that do not factor your community's quality of life or values in their bottom lines. Just say "No" to the sirens.

Dr. Riki Ott shares her personal story of transformation from scientist to democracy activist in Not One Drop, *her second book on the* Exxon Valdez *oil spill (see http://www.rikiott.com/). Ott has appeared in numerous documentaries, including the award-winning feature film,* Black Wave. *She is currently working with national democracy activists on the Campaign to Legalize Democracy through Ultimate Civics, a project of Earth Island Institute (http://www.ultimatecivics. org/), which posts material for the general public and educators from fifth grade through higher education.*

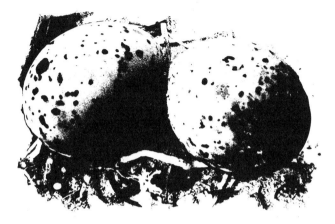

PRICING THE PRICELESS

JESSICA WHEELER

The Pine Island Sound estuary is fed by the Caloosa-hatchee River, which funnels fresh water from Lake Okeechobee to Florida's southwest coast. From above, one can see that the sound is cradled by a ring of delicate barrier islands. Between the barrier islands and the mainland is a constellation of mangrove islands. Each mangrove island is, in turn, dotted with its own constellation of birds—egrets, herons, ibis, pelicans, cormorants, and anhingas. These species nest communally on the islands during the summer, feeding themselves and their young on the bounty of the estuary.

For several summers, I assisted with a study on the nesting success of these birds as part of an internship with J.N. "Ding" Darling National Wildlife Refuge. On one occasion I saw an egret emerge, sodden and helpless, from its egg. I saw the first crack appear and watched the egg move as the tiny bird pecked with amazing force from within. Its beak emerged, and then its head, with streaks of white down clinging damply to its alien-green flesh. I tallied the new hatchling's presence in my field notebook.

After motoring safely back to the mainland, I entered this tally, among many others, into a database. The database stretched back to the 1990s and displayed in vivid graphs the steady decline of wading and diving birds. The decline seemed direct and unstoppable, caused by overdevelopment of the coasts and the impaired water quality that goes with it. Later in 2005, the estuary was besieged with massive amounts of water from the "management" of Lake Okeechobee, approximately 2.9 billion gallons of nutrient-rich fresh water per day. Then Hurricane Charlie hit. One disaster was man-made, the other natural, but together they pushed the ecosystem to the brink. Fish washed up dead on the beaches. Seagrasses and mangroves died. The wading birds, existing near the top of the ecosystem, were negatively impacted as well. The following year, nest success was incredibly low.

Tourists, who traveled from faraway places to see Sanibel Island's magnificent birds, expressed sore disappointment. I was beyond disappointment. I felt betrayed. I had grown up seeing flocks of thousands of egrets, ibis, and roseate spoonbills. I had seen them fish in the murky shallows, their reflections caught in the folds of waves. As disheartening as this decline has been, I feel the estuary is capable of coming back. But not if disturbances continue, day by day, year by year. Like an injured person, the estuary needs time to recuperate before taking on another battle.

A battle like oil.

These estuaries not only tie together Florida's natural environments—providing a link between the terrestrial forests and the plains of seagrass lying below the surface of the water—they also tie together people often otherwise at odds. Fishermen rely on these delicate habitats as nurseries for important commercial and recreational fish species. Together, these species bring in over $6.5 billion every year. Conservationists realize estuaries' value as some of the few remaining nesting areas for threatened wading and diving birds. Those who inhabit the coast value the importance of mangroves and other marshlands in stabilizing the shifting lands of low-lying south Florida. Tourists and locals alike adore the beauty, tranquility, and feeling of awe one gets upon entering a mangrove tunnel or strolling down a pristine beach. And those in the tourist industry know good money when they see it—over $25 billion a year in coastal tourism.

For these reasons, I was shocked to learn that Florida lawmakers were considering oil exploration near one of the most delicate environments on earth, a place where slight changes in salinity, water clarity, and nutrient and pollution levels can throw off the balance of the ecosystem.

I want to know who can look at the sunny expanse of Florida and see potential for oil exploration, rather than the refinement of solar energy. I want to know who thinks jobs will be created at a time when alternative energy sources are America's only hope for future energy independence. We need to admit that the measly amount of oil Florida could contribute would do nothing to lower the price of gas at the pumps. And I want to know who is funding the lobbying that says otherwise.

Beyond this, I want to see Florida legislators stand up to big money. After failing to fight the sugar industry's destructive habits, even with the Everglades at stake, I need to see lawmakers stand up for Florida's coasts.

While we're at it, why don't we talk about costs?

I want my legislators to tell me how much money Florida would make by allowing oil drilling in our pristine waters. Then tell me if they've accounted the cost, both in capital and in ecological damage, of dealing with an oil spill—the cost of cleaning up the oil, the dead birds and fish. Have they accounted for the cost of dune restoration? Seagrass restoration? Oyster reef restoration? Is the attempt to recreate fragile coastal ecosystems included in the estimation of job creation? What about the attempt to reinvigorate confidence in the safety of oil rigs during hurricanes? Could money bring back the tourist industry?

The bill passed by the House would allow oil drilling to occur three to ten miles off the Gulf coast of Florida. Because oil spreads from a spill at an astonishing rate, approximately 197 feet per second, it wouldn't take long for the oil to reach the estuaries, marshes, and beaches. And we cannot pretend an oil spill wouldn't occur in a place that is famous for its hurricane activity. The effects would be devastating.

An oil spill that occurred near the entrance to the Panama Canal in 1986 has been well documented. First, bands of dead mangroves appeared along the coast—their roots, along with the oysters, barnacles, and sponges that live on them, were covered with a suffocating film of oil. Transplanted mangrove seedlings were not able to survive in these polluted areas. Seagrasses in intertidal zones were killed through direct exposure to the oil at low tides. Other seagrass species died off slowly from subsequent algal blooms. Here in Florida, that would mean manatees would have nowhere to graze. Shrimp were killed by the Panama Canal spill and their diminished presence reverberated through the entire food chain. Moreover, once oil enters an estuary, it takes decades for it to be removed.

It doesn't take an actual spill for pollutants to find their way to the water and reach the coast. During normal operation, oil rigs dump toxic drilling fluid, heavy metals, and carcinogens into the oceans, as well as pollute the air much like city traffic. These toxins will not only affect sea life—they will impact those of us who live on, play in, and eat from the Gulf. Should we, as Floridians, believe that the possible gain of oil exploration will outweigh these negative impacts?

I've watched the cycle of life and death in the estuaries. I've seen the estuary nearly destroyed and then, amazingly, recover. I've seen old and young alike awestruck by a fiddler crab clinging to the aerial roots of a mangrove. I've seen thousands of people flock to estuary refuges for one glimpse of the abundance of birds and wildlife thriving there. I've watched a manatee calf follow her meandering mother through the beds of healthy seagrass. I've watched dolphins jump for sheer joy. I've seen the exuberant face of a child after catching her first sheepshead.

Ding Darling National Wildlife Refuge fell to pieces after the discharged water from Lake Okeechobee and the lashing winds of Hurricane Charlie. With time, patience, and the loving dedication of Florida's citizens, the estuary is almost back. Maybe we'll never again see the abundance of birds and wildlife documented by the pioneers of Florida; maybe the fisheries will always be a shadow of what they once were. But, if we take care now, maybe we can preserve them as they are today. Maybe, if we fight big issues like coastal development and oil, we can hold on to these idyllic scenes.

Florida's coasts are not a place. They are a way of life. They symbolize both natural and man-made prosperity. I know I speak for millions when I say that Florida is who I am. Taking advantage of Florida's precious coasts for the sake of temporary monetary gain destroys the people who love this state for what it is—paradise.

Jessica Wheeler recently graduated from New College of Florida with a degree in ecology. She is currently at Archbold Biological Station in central Florida, where she studies an endangered scrub mint, chases cows, and sings songs about Florida. Her writing career is just beginning.

THE GULF OF GENERATIONS

MANDIE RAINWATER

When I was ten my parents moved our family from North Carolina, the only home I had ever known, down to the small town of Brooksville, Florida. The long drive through Georgia in the moving truck incited in me a childish anticipation of the adventures that lay ahead—I imagined scenes from *Flipper* and *Hawaii 5-0*, the only "Florida" I knew. When we arrived, my hopes and dreams were crushed. Cookie-cutter houses sat in the middle of what to me was the largest sandbox in the world. Grass might have grown on the land at one point, but not anymore. I was instantly homesick. I longed for North Carolina, for the colors of the trees and the cool gusts that rustled the branches.

Rain came two days after we arrived. After the hardest of the rain hit, the wind began to blow, and with it came the scent of salt. The perfumed breeze delivered my first whiff of ocean, and all of my senses came alive. I bugged my father to drive me toward the smell, toward the Gulf of Mexico. I had been to the shores of the Atlantic before, but this body of water was different. The TV shows had implied that the Gulf was the bluest water anywhere, and now I would be the judge of that.

We got into our Dodge and headed west. A few dead-ends and U-turns and, at my mother's insistence, one stop for directions found us following a long, two-lane road into what felt like a trap. There were no pull-offs in sight, and "Caution Alligator" signs every quarter mile added to our fear of the unknown.

Then, as if transported through time, we were let out of the sawgrass-lined asphalt onto an ancient, unspoiled stretch of beach with the whitest sand I had ever seen. The sun reflected off a calm Gulf, making a mirror of its surface. The bright reflection hit our eyes, causing my father to slam on the brakes and curse under his breath.

He navigated into a narrow parking spot in the crude lot, trying to avoid a puddle that potentially hid a massive pothole. "Everyone out! And don't hit the cars next to us!" he shouted as he turned off the engine, not noticing that we were alone. We filed out in silence, afraid to say anything and in awe of the natural wonder that we had stumbled upon. We took two folding chairs and a bag of towels from the trunk and walked toward the silken sand, passing a sign that said "Pine Island Preserve." I walked the fastest, heading straight for the azure water, pulled to it like a compass needle to magnetic north.

The air had warmed since the shower and I anticipated the chill of the Gulf water. I shed my shoes and clothing and dashed boldly in. The water was warm, and I slowed, trying not to disturb the sand with my feet. Glints of silver darted back and forth, becoming large schools of baby fish as my eyes adjusted. I saw the occasional crab scurry when I moved small patches of slick seaweed with my toes. My mother yelled my name and pointed away from shore. Four dolphins jumped and played, and in my naiveté I waited for one of them to walk on its tail backwards across the water.

We lived in the sandbox a few months before my parents found a small place twenty miles away on a human-made island in Weeki Wachee Springs. There, Florida's Gulf Coast stole my heart forever from the mountains of my birth. From the banks of the Weeki Wachee River I witnessed a manatee give birth to her calf and an alligator in a death spin. I spent lazy Saturdays fishing with Walter, the crane that thought he was a human. I boated with my family from the river into the Gulf to fish and look for dolphins. We drove south to Tampa and fished off of the Sunshine Skyway, the grandest bridge I have ever crossed. We explored Clearwater, Indian Rocks, Dunedin, and Saint Petersburg.

The Gulf looked bluer at each new shoreline and seemed to expand forever. My imagination flourished with thoughts of pirates, whales, crackens, and mermaids. In fact, I was going to be a mermaid when I grew up. Weeki Wachee Springs was home to many young ladies and men over the years who donned tails and performed underwater as mermaids and mermen for tourists. I practiced every chance I got, swimming with my legs tied together as far as I could go without breathing.

I was almost old enough to attend Weeki Wachee's summer training camp for girls when my father told us we were moving back to North Carolina. My grandfather was ill. We left two weeks later, none of us wanting to go. I was almost twelve.

As I grew I remembered fondly those years along the shores of the Gulf, and I often refer to those short years as my childhood. My family always spoke of moving back. My mother insisted that after my brother and I moved out she and my father would return. She passed away before she could do that, but included in her eulogy was a poem that I wrote that placed her home on the shores of Pine Island. Her ashes were scattered off of the Sunshine Skyway, the grandest bridge she had ever crossed.

I returned to the home of my childhood at thirty, with children of my own. I am teaching them that the Gulf is a world unto itself. If they intend to show their children the white beaches and wild dolphins, it is up to each of us to keep the Gulf and her treasures unspoiled. When my ashes are released from the Sunshine Skyway, I want to drift on gentle breezes, down onto crystal blue waters, and become the mermaid of my dreams.

Mandie Rainwater is a full-time, nontraditional student at Florida Gulf Coast University where she is a secondary education major. She is married with two children and is an active volunteer with C.A.R.E.S. Suicide Prevention. Mandie also contributes to the opinion section of the FGCU student newspaper, Eagle News.

DRILLING FOR TROUBLE

ELLIE ALEXANDRA LEVY

My grandfather, Rick Lane, was an oil driller from 1966 to 1983, and by the end of his career he was recognized as one of the best oil drillers in the state of California. He knows the good, the bad, the ins, and the outs of the business. He knows the truth, he knows the horrors.

As a driller on an offshore rig, my grandfather saw the mistakes that could be made and the harm that could be done, both to his colleagues and to the environment.

"People make mistakes," Grandpa said to me. "Accidents are inevitable, so we should just keep them minimal."

My grandfather explained to me how "drilling mud" is pumped through a drill pipe to keep the drilling equipment lubricated. The workers would fill up barrels with either oil-based or water-based mud. When the mud reached the bottom of the pipe it got pushed back up, along with clippings from the drill bit. The men would occasionally let too much oil out by one of myriad mistakes, such as opening the wrong valve. According to my grandfather, about half of oil-based mud is toxic, and accidents ranged anywhere from spilling ten percent to 100 percent of the mud. Other times the men were told to spill the excess water-based mud into the ocean in the middle of the night. Although it was not as toxic as mud that was oil-based, it was still hazardous to the aquatic environment.

In our conversation, my grandfather shared the tragic stories of his friends and co-workers who were seriously injured on the job. One day, the casing of a large pipe crashed down on a worker's foot. The pipe had a thick rubber base. Because of the rubber, the pipe was not sharp or strong, so when it landed it didn't slice the foot in a clean cut. It crushed it.

My grandfather remembers the deaths especially. Once he and a co-worker were screwing pipes together. Suddenly, the pipe hit and broke off the stabbing board. The stabbing board is a temporary platform meant to remain twenty to forty feet above the ground. Its purpose is solely to act as a place for the drillers to work on. Suddenly, the stabbing board, appropriately named, split in half and swung straight down toward the ground and stabbed my grandfather's co-worker directly in his chest. The puncture killed him instantly.

Another tragedy occurred when a driller lifted a fifteen-foot pipe too high, causing it to snap a line of piping. The pipe swung around and sliced the man's head clean off.

My grandfather wasn't spared injury. He often carried heavy objects to the welding truck in order for the object to be repaired. Once he was taking a pipe from a section of the pump to the truck. The pipe was about six to eight inches across and was L-shaped. When he put the pipe down, my grandfather's finger got caught in the end of the truck and was sliced off.

The tragedies aren't caused only by equipment mishaps. The men are working at a very high elevation on a rig. Once, my grandfather remembers, while his crew was moving the rig, he was asked to dismantle it with large trucks and cranes. At an extraordinarily high altitude, he took a sledgehammer and knocked off pins that were roughly six inches long and four inches thick. Knocking the last pin out, he thought everything was fine until he was thrown from the crane. Luckily, my grandfather had a safety belt on and fell only twenty feet. However, the belt got caught and crashed him into the rig. He hit his leg so hard it swelled seven inches larger than the other leg. He was one of the lucky ones, because most of the time the men did not wear their safety belts, since they felt the belts slowed them down.

These are only a few of the extraordinary number of stories that can be told by a single worker. There are also perpetual and chronic health issues that are instigated by chemical exposure. My grandfather has developed a blood condition, called neutropenia, because of his time on the rig. His immune system does not have an adequate amount of white blood cells to fight infection. Doctors say that he got the disease from all of the chemicals that he mixed to treat the mud. He is on medication, which has side effects such as bone and muscle pain, headaches, nausea, nosebleeds, and vomiting—just another cost of doing business. Even after all these years, Rick Lane is proof that time does not heal all.

On top of the extreme dangers that drillers face, subtle issues plague them long afterwards, emotional issues. One cannot neglect to acknowledge the devastating effects that oil rig work has on a driller's mental health. The emotional well-being of workers is most often in a turbulent state, as the workers are away from their loved ones for long periods of time. Alcoholism and depression are rampant among these men. My grandfather saw and experienced the serious psychological consequences of life on an oil rig and admitted it "wasn't exactly a pretty picture."

The reality is that oil drilling is dangerous not just for the environment but for the drillers as well. Given the scarce nature of the job market, I understand the argument that oil drilling in the Gulf would be a wonderful way to provide people with much-needed work. But I believe that, faced with these stories, most people and their families would agree that their safety and their lives are far more important than a paycheck.

Ellie Alexandra Levy is an eighteen-year-old freshman in the honors program at Florida Gulf Coast University. Outside of her education, she is professionally dedicated to service. She is the representative for the Reach for the Stars Foundation, benefiting individuals with cystic fibrosis. Writing from her dorm and speaking at events are the two main ways that she represents the foundation and the causes that she believes in.

SANCTUARY

A. JAMES WOHLPART

I live and work in the busy-ness of southwest Florida, between the western edge of the River of Grass and the magical beaches of Sanibel Island. Tamiami Trail, the eight-laned heart of Lee County, courses through strip malls with vacant shops, past desolate car dealerships, sentinels to a bygone era of cheap oil, and gated communities with Niagara-like fountains guarding grandiose entrances degraded with signs that shout, "Reduced! Lakefront living from the 200s!"

Interstate 75, in the process of being six-laned, once separated development to the west from lands to the east reserved for aquifer recharge, panthers, swallow-tailed kites, and all things wild. But with the boom of the 1990s and early 2000s, even the protected lands in the eastern part of the county sprawl with shopping malls and isolated communities that popped up like dollar weed on an overwatered lawn. Most neighborhoods now sport empty homes with the all-too-familiar signs taped on their windows ("Foreclosure!" "Warning! Do Not Enter!") and lawns being reclaimed by weeds.

We drive everywhere in southwest Florida, often as fast as we can. When forced to, we sit idle at stoplights that are sometimes less than a half mile apart, listening to engines rattle and breathing noxious fumes from exhaust pipes. We meander down roads that take us far out of our way to get to the next store or post office or friend's home or place of work, evidence of a lack of urban planning that continued right on through the boom. As a result of this shortsightedness, we consume more than our fair share of gas and oil. We participate in a culture and an economy built on short-term goals, on how to extract the most out of precious Earth in the quickest way possible without thinking about what comes next or who or what gets edged out. All our progress— our Hummers and McMansions and sprawling urban development that eats up land like some ravenous beast— has created a world of distraction that empties our spirits and leaves us hungering for something more, something real.

On rare occasions, I escape west, to the Gulf of Mexico and the pristine beaches of Sanibel Island. After passing through the toll plaza and beginning the drive across the causeway, I begin to slow. The smell of salty spray induces me to roll down my windows and turn off the air conditioner. Sun glints off the waves that flow across the bay in an undulating rhythm that is part of something larger, the pull of the moon, winds that have circulated across continents, our rolling, rotating Earth.

Sanibel's unspoiled beaches are known throughout the world for their shells, yet what is less well-known is that the island is a sanctuary where humans have agreed to curtail their behavior in order to live in harmony with wildlife. It offers a way of living that flows with the natural world, that emanates out of the rhythms of nature, that is in tune with the hum of creation.

I find my way to the beach and greet the sparkling Gulf. The warm sun kisses my skin, the salty air cleanses my lungs, the waves press against the shoreline, undulating, rocking. I remember my small place in the much grander universe. I remember that we can live by ideals more noble than those prescribed by the progress of mankind, that a tune is being played throughout this vast and magical universe and that a worthy life goal would be to live and work and play and love in harmony with that tune.

As a sanctuary, Sanibel Island, like all the islands that stretch from Key West through the Big Bend on up to the Panhandle, cradles the human spirit, reminding us of all our relations and reviving in us a longing to be better people, to become balanced and whole. I remember that there is more to life than getting and spending, that true happiness comes from something more than bigger and faster cars, that my culture must find a way to embrace long-term solutions to enduring problems. I sense that I have a moral obligation to future generations and that the choices I make today must take into consideration my great-great-grandchildren's great-grandchildren.

On the shore of the magical and mysterious Gulf of Mexico, I connect with something deeper and richer, something that sparks a remembering in me of a different time, a different way of being filled with slowness and foresight, and, for a short time, I am home.

A. James Wohlpart is professor of environmental literature and associate dean in the College of Arts and Sciences at Florida Gulf Coast University. He is coeditor of A Voice for Earth: American Writers Respond to the Earth Charter. *He has lived and worked, hiked, canoed, and kayaked in southwest Florida for over fifteen years.*

ISLANDS OF FREEDOM

KATHRYN KEENE WOHLPART

When I was young, I got the chance to do things that opened me to nature. I got to see the beauty that embraces us as humans. I got to feel the freedom that can only be found in a child who has opened her eyes on a beautiful beach. I hiked with my parents and felt the sun warm my skin. I read about adventures that weren't my own, yet I shared them with the narrator. I swam in an ocean deeper than imagination itself.

The first clear memory I have of this taste of freedom took place on Cayo Costa. My brother's Boy Scout troop went on a camping trip and I got to go along with my father. It rained all day and into the night. That evening we gathered around a bonfire. All of the parents were cooking something, which I couldn't see, thanks to the lovely tarp that was protecting me from being drenched. Then, as if by magic, a slice of warm berry pie appeared in front of me.

The next day, the rain let up and I started exploring the island. I inched away from camp, pushing myself to go farther and farther, to ignore my fear of being lost. Then, I let myself imagine. I imagined people walking with me, able to see everything as I saw it. I imagined people in the world being able to see a beauty called Mother Nature. I imagined flying above the island, seeing it the way the birds did.

My fears completely dissipated. By playing this imaginary game on a magical, remote island, I set my soul free. I wasn't just a child whose words were sometimes ignored. I was a soul, soaring higher and higher. When I landed in my body again, I looked about and saw things I had not noticed. I felt as if I could really see.

I built a fort, just a simple one. It was small, only big enough for me to sit in, one wall of fronds stacked against a branch. My dad happily snapped a picture. Looking at that photo now, I see that he caught in my toothless grin the exact face of freedom, a freedom I still carry with me as I continue to grow.

On that day, on that miraculous island, there were no worries, no sense of time passing, just deep magic. I suppose that there is a time in everyone's life where everything stands still, as it did for me that day. I remember the slowness of the day, my breathing in and out. In that moment I was so deeply connected to everything, I became connected to myself.

Another time, I remember spending a day in my backyard with a tarp spread between two pine trees. At the end of the day, when my dad was helping me untie the ropes from the trees he instructed me to give each tree a hug. I refused, not understanding why I would want to do such a thing. He simply told me that the tree loved me enough to hold shade over me and endure the rope being tied to it. He told me that the tree had earned a hug, but if I didn't want to give it one, that was fine too. I waited outside, staring at the tree in shock, after my father had gone inside. I hadn't pictured a tree's feelings before.

I rushed up to each tree in the yard and hugged it. "Thank you!" I thought. "Thank you, thank you, thank you."

To be able to reach these moments of love and clarity, one has to be in the right place. I have been lucky. Close to my home in Fort Myers I have found many places that connected me to the world and therefore to myself.

Even closer to home than Cayo Costa was the beach. My brother and I had a simple blow-up raft. On weekdays it was nothing special, just something that sat in our garage. When the weekend came, that simple little raft became our vessel to a whole new world. The drive out to Sanibel was almost agonizing as the car inched slowly toward our private world.

We soared! Drifting over the water, we wondered what world we would be entering next. We had no cares, no worries, at least until it was time to leave. Even then I knew that the beach would still be there the next weekend. I knew that when I was older I would be able to come back and walk along those same beaches where I had once played.

Now, I'm not so sure.

It's hard to think of what might happen to my home. To picture the blue water and white sands transformed. To see all of those places where my generation played and laughed, gone. To see the islands of our freedom, our innocent and carefree childhoods, disappear.

To see the beauty lost.

I don't want my home to become a story of what humans did wrong. I can't bear to sit and have all that has become sacred in my life disrupted.

We don't have the right to make this unspoiled place a thing of the past. We don't own nature. No one owns nature. Nature is owned by a collective community of different species, including future generations of plants and animals. What we do must take them into account.

Kathryn Keene "Kat" Wohlpart is in her sophomore year at Estero High School, where she is in the marching band. She is taking advanced placement and honors courses in English, environmental science, European history, chemistry, and algebra II. She moved to southwest Florida when she was three months old and has lived there ever since.

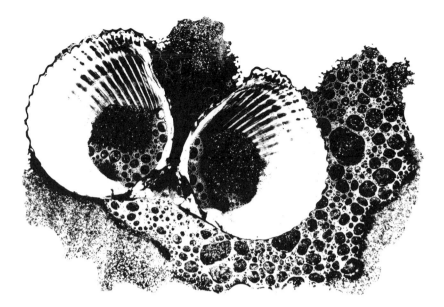

A FERAL BEAUTY

MYRA MENDIBLE

My husband and I lived on Sanibel during my year's sabbatical, trading the bright lights, busy streets, and urban bustle of inner-city Miami for an island just beyond the reach of mainland development. At the time, we knew little about life on Sanibel beyond what we'd seen in tourist brochures. We knew that Sanibel had long been a favorite vacation destination for snow birds seeking temporary relief from intemperate northern climes, and that it had earned an international reputation for the variety of shells found along stretches of its private white sand beaches. What we didn't know was that Sanibel would inspire, surprise, and delight us in ways that were far from trivial or temporary.

Restricted public lighting and building codes on the island (nothing over three stories high) have produced an unexpected side-effect: the nights are so dark that I found myself planning my evenings in sync with the stages of the moon. A full moon granted me an evening stroll on the beach, a quarter-moon made it harder to spot the eight-foot alligator who often wandered into our yard from the lake behind our house. This city girl with an aversion to sentimentality or pathos found herself so captivated by the number and brightness of stars gracing Sanibel's night sky that romantic clichés about starry nights—the bane of writing teachers everywhere—now assumed a freshness and truth. Stranger still was my reaction to the lack of street lights. I'd always been afraid of the dark, yet I have never again felt as safe as I did when shrouded in Sanibel's still, dark night.

We grew accustomed to the sound of the sea, to watching fish hawks hunt in the lake behind the house, to flocks of white ibises foraging in the grass, to alligators sunning themselves in the midday sun—giant lizards in some B-movie I'd seen as a child. I ran on the beach early in the mornings, hearing only the wind, my breathing, and the splashing of fish feeding at dawn. Once, as I took greedy breaths of sea air to finish the morning mile, I caught sight of something extraordinary—a mass migration of stingrays—thousands of them swimming in file along miles of shallow water. I was transfixed, grateful for the honor of bearing witness to a primordial ritual, a natural rite of passage that has ensured survival. In this place the sea casts its beautiful bones on the sand each day; every afternoon, I harvested coquinas, tulips, lightning whelks, and olive shells, marveling at their otherworldliness. The sea's gifts to me became my gifts to others, as shells then graced mirrors and shadow boxes, my handmade offerings to friends and family.

Even our urban cats, Peanuts and Love Puss, once adept at dodging cars on neighborhood streets, delighted in this wild and unspoiled new environment. The orange tabby, Peanuts, had been the bane of sparrows, so we made him wear a collar with bells to warn his feathered prey. But when he encountered a great blue heron for the first time, our little predator bolted, confused and terrified at the sight of a bird over four feet tall. It wasn't unusual for raccoons, turtles, or groups of sleek bobcats about knee-high to travel through our backyard at night. One evening, we heard a cat yelp and ran outside. Flashlight in hand, my husband found himself face-to-face with a full-grown bobcat. He had thick forelegs, pointy ears, and our precious Love Puss dangling from his mouth. My husband did something that he'd later marvel at and could not explain: he knelt down on one knee and met the big cat's yellow eyes. They stared at each other for a long moment, then that splendid animal did something surprising as well: he dropped our dead cat, turned, and was gone in one graceful leap over our neighbor's fence.

We buried Love Puss by the lake, deep in the soil that nourishes such abundant life in Sanibel. The gumbo limbo tree we planted in his memory has grown tall and shades our new home. That year we spent on Sanibel enriched our lives immeasurably, and we came to understand that there was a price to pay for its feral beauty: a debt we owe the natural world. Those of us who have known the joy of Sanibel's magnificent coast, its natural bounty and unique gifts, have made a silent promise to honor that debt.

Myra Mendible is professor of English and chair of the Literature and Languages Department at Florida Gulf Coast University. She has published widely in a variety of peer-reviewed journals and is the editor of an interdisciplinary collection of essays, From Bananas to Buttocks: The Latina Body in Popular Film and Culture. *Her most recent collection,* Race 2008: Critical Reflections on an Historic Election, *will be published in 2010.*

GANAWENIA
NIMAMAINAN AKI

OANNES ARTHUR PRITZKER

For more than a millennium, ancient culture peoples of Florida—the Calusa, Tequesta, Timuca, Togobagan, Appalachee, Tallahasee, and other smaller tribes—lived in a harmonious relationship with the sea. Like contemporary indigenous peoples throughout the world, those ancient native cultures had a reverence for sea life, which provided much of their very subsistence. Like contemporary indigenous peoples, the ancient culture tribes had a deep cultural and spiritual relationship with the oceans. Anything that would threaten or harm the marine environment was unthinkable. It was a serious violation of tribal law.

The world we live in is at a critical time in our planet's history because we have violated this ethic. Many serious problems confronting humanity come from anthropogenic causes, including especially the use of fossil fuels which threatens our global climate.

Oceans are an integral part of our planet's biosphere. Their role and influence on global climate and regional weather systems are well known to the scientific community. Marine biochemistry is delicately balanced and can easily be disrupted by oil and gas exploration and production. The degraded water chemistry results in killing of sea life. Significantly, the poisoning of the marine food chain does not wait for the actual development, does not depend on an *Exxon Valdez* spill; rather, it begins during the energy exploration phase and then grows steadily.

In my native Wabanaki culture, we have an expression, "Ganawenia Nimamainan Aki," which means "respect our Mother Earth." This concept is at odds with the value system of industrial society. The energy industry seems only to value money and profit. They do not care about respecting our Mother Earth. They do not care about healthy fisheries, sea turtles, wading birds, clean beaches, or even the humans who rely on the ocean's ecological functions. They only care about making a profit for their CEOs and their boards.

The ocean, to coastal indigenous peoples, is not just a major seafood source that nutritionally sustains us. The ocean, to contemporary native peoples, is not just a source of revenue. The ocean is a central part of our territories and our cultural and spiritual life-ways.

The web of life that marine biologists term "fisheries" is, to native peoples, our relative. We say in my native language, "Kinonwanatquasin," "all of our relations." My Wabanaki culture and those of other tribal peoples believe that all life, including marine life, has a spirit. This is why indigenous peoples perform ceremonies to show reverence and respect to the ocean. At the beginning of our fishing season, the community gathers at a sacred place along the coast where our spiritual leaders guide everyone in a prayer ceremony to the ocean.

In my youth, I remember being instructed in various drum songs that honored our fish and marine relatives. These songs are still sung today. I was also taught that when I set off from shore I should give a small pinch of sweet grass or native tobacco from my prayer pouch as an offering to the spirits of our marine life relatives. This personal ceremony is a way of asking permission of our fish relatives that we may catch a few of them in order for us to live. Elders from different native communities talk about speaking with sincerity to the waters so that the marine life will hear our appreciation as we hunt and fish them. In many native languages, words used to describe a marine species, be it a cod or salmon, a quahaug clam, seal, whale, crab, or type of seaweed, are spoken in a context that suggests that each species has its own family and is therefore related to our tribal family.

Tribal laws and codes of conduct that are monitored and enforced by clan mothers ensure that we "harvest" only the amount of marine life needed for our subsistence. Indigenous people's paradigm would never allow for overfishing. Taking more than necessary was abhorrent to my "Nichitanganooks," "my ancestors," who first saw how those from far other places, or as we say in my native language, the "Wampiskitunk," had no regard for Mother Earth and Kinonwantaquasin, all of our relations, our natural world relatives.

Florida's ancient culture peoples, as well as the Seminole, Miccosukee, and Yuchi-Creek of a later date, could not have believed that there would be a time when many fisheries would reach the point of collapse. That time is now here; the Gulf of Mexico is a very tragic example. Dead zones; commercial overfishing; and damage and destruction of fragile seagrass beds, coral reefs, mangrove forests, and barrier islands by a multitude of causes have created a critical state in Florida. These unique coastal zones serve as vital nursery habitat for most every species of marine life. The biological recovery and long-term sustainability of finfish and shellfish populations, especially those of major economic importance, is in serious jeopardy.

In the Gulf of Mexico, this situation is primarily due to physical loss of habitat from development, as well as from toxic water pollution. Contamination of estuaries from agricultural, industrial, and urban waste runoff is a major culprit.

Energy development is another serious reason for the death and decline of marine life. Oil and gas exploration and production use voluminous amounts of highly toxic drilling fluids. These "muds" along with waste oil are washed off the energy rigs as poisonous effluent. This, combined with numerous so-called "small" oil spills that routinely occur from pipelines and ship traffic, is a recipe for disaster. Oil development in the Gulf of Mexico should be considered a crime against the people of Florida, not to mention a crime against the environment.

Contemporary native peoples are shocked and upset by the many abuses being done to Mother Earth, especially to the world's oceans. Since early contact with the "Wampiskitunk," translated as "people from across the waters" and meaning primarily Euro-Americans, indigenous peoples throughout the world have made numerous efforts to warn the greedy industrial society of the ecological consequences to our biosphere and to humanity from disrespecting and mistreating the planet. Anthropogenic impacts to the climate that affect our oceans is one of the most frightening and serious problems.

Global climate change from our dependence on fossil fuels is now a twenty-first-century threat to the world's oceans and thereby to everyone on the planet. Scientists have documented sea temperature fluctuations that are known to be killing tropical coral reefs and affecting fragile polar marine environments. The 2009 United Nations Climate Summit in Copenhagen, Denmark, as well as many other previous global forums, have heard much testimony about changes to weather and ocean currents and what are current and probable impacts.

As an indigenous person, an ecologist, and a resident of Florida, I am concerned about the future health of the Gulf of Mexico if oil and gas development is permitted. Further development of fossil fuels is antithetical to indigenous people's ways of kinship and harmony. It is also unnecessary when clean, safe, efficient, and affordable renewable energy sources such as solar, wind, ocean current, geo-thermal, and sustainable bio-fuels like algae can provide equitable energy for everyone on earth.

My Nichitanganooks, my ancestors, warned about a time in human history when greed would run rampant, and humans would act with complete disregard for the well-being of contemporary and future generations of all life. The raping of the planet for energy, as exemplified in the development of oil and gas in the Gulf of Mexico, is a tragic fulfillment of this ancient indigenous prophecy. It is not too late if all of us who have reverence for Mother Earth, who have respect and concern for our oceans, stand up against this insane value system that puts dollars before dolphins, profit for a small few before a clean and healthy environment for all, a value system that ignores the science behind climate change and holds no concern for our future.

Oannes Arthur Pritzker was director of the Yat Kitischee Native Center, an inter-tribal cultural, social justice, environmental, and news media organization. Oannes was a highly respected Native American ecologist, journalist, and educator. He spent much of his life protecting our planet's biosphere and defending human rights and promoting social justice throughout the world. He passed on to his creator just before the Deepwater Horizon explosion.

It has been said that indigenous cultures feel the rending of Mother Earth, sometimes long before the rupture becomes apparent to others. Perhaps we should consider Oannes' passing as a telling sign that what we have done to Mother Earth has simply been too much. Oannes was a great teacher and friend to many. He will be missed.

THE SCIENCE
OF CLIMATE CHANGE
IN THE
TEN THOUSAND ISLANDS

MICHAEL SAVARESE

AND

SASHA LINSIN WOHLPART

The Ten Thousand Islands is one of the few remaining regions of undeveloped Florida coast. Located south and east of Marco Island and extending to Everglades City, the region is aptly named for its numerous, mangrove-forest islands. They exist principally as the consequence of two phenomena: a modest rate of sea-level rise and the growth and reproduction of the lowly oyster.

The Eastern oyster, *Crassostrea virginica*, in addition to being a culinary delight, is coastal southwest Florida's premier architect. Through the animal's feeding, it induces sedimentation by trapping mud, and through the animal's growth and reproduction, oysters congregate on the floors of estuarine bays. The two, mud trapping and growth, generate reef structure.

At the same time, sea level is rising. Rate of sea-level rise over the last 3,500 years has been relatively modest, less than 10 centimeters per century. Under such rates, oysters are able to win the proverbial horse race—reef sedimentation exceeds sea-level rise and the reefs eventually become emergent at low tides.

Once exposed at low tide, red mangrove propagules settle, take root, and a forested island is born. Repeat this ten thousand times and a coastal geomorphology becomes apparent: a vast collection of thin, connected mangrove islands that create a labyrinth of estuarine passageways and bays.

But if the dynamics of the horse race change, and the sea-level-rise pony becomes a strong finisher, a different outcome is predicted. When the rate of sea-level rise exceeds oyster sedimentation, the natural succession of reef to mangrove-forested island is disturbed. Because of this, climate change has regional import—global warming has accelerated the rate of sea-level rise, perhaps beyond the oyster's capacity to keep pace.

The planet's sea level is dynamic and has changed significantly through geological time, even without the presence of humans. In recent history, however, extremes of natural variation have been exacerbated by human activity. The burning of fossil fuels has caused a significant increase in atmospheric carbon dioxide. This in turn has increased the greenhouse potential of the atmosphere, and the rate of sea-level rise has increased substantially. Our current rate of rise, approximately 35 centimeters per century, is an order of magnitude higher than it was during the time the Ten Thousand Islands were conceived. The rules governing the islands' existence haven't changed; rather, the poker table has turned in favor of the house.

The Ten Thousand Islands owes its natural state to the fact that it is owned largely by the state and federal governments. The upstream watersheds are protected by public ownership as well, allowing for the capture of rainwater that ultimately moves into the Ten Thousand Islands' estuaries. Unlike developed portions of the southwest Florida coast, where urban and suburban construction form a barrier to habitat migration, the effects of sea-level rise on the land- and estuarine-scape can play out naturally in the Ten Thousand Islands. Vegetative habitats can migrate without interference, and patterns of sedimentation can alter coastal geomorphology. The islands therefore serve as a natural laboratory for the study of sea-level effects on the coast.

The response of coastal geomorphology to the increased rate of sea-level rise has revealed that coasts don't simply react in a linear and orderly fashion. They don't march back landward in an obvious and predictable manner. Rather, coasts behave dynamically, disorderly. When people in southwest Florida talk about sea-level rise they often joke about finally being able to afford beachfront property. Governmental agencies and managers often draft maps repositioning the coastline at the topographic contour for a given magnitude sea-level position—a three-foot rise in sea level means all property under a three foot elevation is under water, and property just slightly higher can expect dramatic sunsets across the Gulf's horizon. Unfortunately, it's not that simple, nor that predictable.

The Ten Thousand Islands provide clues. The waters most conducive for oyster growth and reproduction are no longer in the bays immediately adjacent to the mainland, where the submerged area for reef development is greatest. Rather, the location of best oyster health is now positioned farther upstream in the lower reaches of the rivers, where habitation space for oysters is limited.

The sedimentation rate of reefs within the bays has been

lowered considerably, making it less capable of keeping pace with sea-level rise. Inland of the inner bays can be found the marginal mangrove forest. This forest can be three miles wide, and its position demarks the furthest incursion of tidal influence. Sea-level rise has shifted the distribution of mangroves sporadically across the landscape so that they now invade areas once dominated by more inland marsh grasses, sedges, and rushes. Most interesting, though, is the deflation of marsh elevations in certain areas. The organic peaty soils that underlie the marshes can decay rapidly and cause abrupt drops in elevation. This has led to the formation of "pocks," which eventually merge to form brackish water ponds and bays.

In essence, an incipient estuary is being created well landward of the current Ten Thousand Island bays. This is a coast that is altering from the inside out. It's not a landscape that anyone is preparing for and not one for which management practices are attuned. Beachfront property and glorious sunsets will not necessarily come to those who wait.

Global industrialization has encouraged coastal development for at most one thousand years, all during an interval of geological history when sea-level rise rate was slight, protected estuaries developed, and humans could take advantage of the estuarine bounty and protection. Society is not accustomed to a high rate of sea-level rise. In fact, the juxtaposition of the right conditions to promote estuary formation is a rarity, the exception rather than the rule throughout geological time.

One could argue that the planet's changes should run their course regardless of the effects humans might impose. There's a real social and economic cost to bear with that decision, however. The more prudent would argue that the impending impacts of sea-level rise upon our coasts are premature, that it's not time for estuaries and coasts to succumb to sea-level rise, that nature hadn't intended for these impacts to arrive at this juncture in history. Such a change would have a profound impact on our way of life in southwest Florida.

Significantly, society has the power and the technology to mitigate the rate of change. The power resides in our willingness to return the composition of our atmosphere to a more natural state by changing human behavior. The Ten Thousand Islands should merit its name for millennia to come. Future generations should be permitted to experience and enjoy its splendor.

Michael Savarese is a professor of marine science and Director of Graduate Studies at Florida Gulf Coast University. He has published numerous papers concerning restoration science and the history of coastal change. He is very active in the community helping to inform the public about climate change and works closely with environmental agencies to develop effective management strategies and policies. Southwest Florida and the Greater Everglades have been his home for the last fifteen years.

Sasha Linsin Wohlpart is an instructor in the Department of Marine and Ecological Sciences at Florida Gulf Coast University. Her graduate research focused on estuarine development in southwest Florida and she continues to explore this topic through her scholarship activities and teaching. She has lived in Florida and explored its beaches, wetlands, and uplands for the past 27 years.

THE GREAT BLUE RIVER
BILL BELLEVILLE

I have been scuba diving for years now, and the mysteries of the sea that have come to most captivate me are not the large sharks or the sea turtles or even the giant rays that glide through the water like prehistoric birds. Instead, it is the coral polyp and the great castles of limerock it builds for itself.

It is for this reason I often go into the ocean at twilight, just as the polyp—looking like a tiny anemone—emerges from its scup in the star and brain and elkhorn coral to feed. It does so by capturing plankton, specks of plants and animals that ride oceanic currents.

Once a year, by late summer, these same corals will also bulge with great promise in the full blackness of the night. That promise is realized as an annual spawn in which eggs—or packets of eggs and sperm—push up from each polyp until they pulse just at the surface of the reef.

Then, when nature plays a secret chord, the eggs and packets burst at once from their limerock castle, as if fired by a volley of tiny militia. The sea around me will be filled with new life, and these tiny miracles and all they portend will float away with the current. They will drift until the precise moment when the egg transforms to animal and forever sinks to the bottom, where a new reef will be born.

Corals have been building reefs like this for nearly 400 million years. But, as usual, we land mammals are just now catching on. It wasn't until the early eighteenth century that a French scientist discovered coral wasn't a plant at all—nor was it a rock, as some believed. Indeed, it was a very complex animal so delicate it could be stressed by a change of a few degrees, or by a few milligrams of toxins.

It's great irony that just as we are now learning about our corals, we are also in jeopardy of losing them: reefs in the Florida Keys and offshore Southeast Florida have been declining in health over the last twenty to thirty years because of human impacts—from nutrient loading to ship groundings to overfishing.

There is, of course, some good news in that we're also learning to repopulate ailing reefs with grafts of live coral. And with a new awareness of how upland pollutants find their way downstream to the shallow reefs, we're trying to improve the water quality that sustains the coral animals.

This knowledge is critical since the reefs here underpin an economy that—according to a Florida Fish and Wildlife Conservation Commission study—results in $4.3 billion a year in tourism and fisheries. Other benefits, such as creating an underwater limerock berm that keeps our islands from washing away, are difficult to fully appreciate, but are no less real.

As for context, it helps to know our reefs occupy less than one half of one percent of our oceans here on this "Blue Planet." Yet they nurture a great menagerie of animals that spend time there feeding, breeding, resting, and hiding.

In Florida, coral reefs and the currents that affect them have been woven into written maritime history from the very first: explorer Juan Ponce DeLeon paid close attention since they affected navigation and could also provide food. DeLeon also "discovered" a strong current that surged out of the Gulf of Mexico and, after confluxing with other powerful oceanic drifts, became the "Gulf Stream."

This Stream could be used to carry galleons and corsairs up the Florida coast and send them back to the Old World. As a diver, I sometimes ride this current myself on "drift dives" off West Palm Beach, twitching my fins in the three-knot current to steer, not needing to do much else.

The icon of Key West literary history, Ernest Hemingway, once wrote of taking his boat out into "the great blue river" to fish for marlin and swordfish. "Papa" may not have seen a coral reef in its annual nocturnal spawn, but I'm guessing he understood the sways of the currents and tides very well. He surely saw the way both the terrestrial keys—as well as the reefs—were sliced into "spur and groove" formations because the upstream currents had surged through them for so long. The knowledge of that was unmistakable, etched deeply into the dry limerock and submerged corals.

And now, there are those politicians and oil industry shills who would allow near-shore oil drilling in the Gulf and the Florida Straits. They argue new sources of domestic crude will make Florida more prosperous and, of course, keep us "nationally secure."

This is a terrifically specious argument since it doesn't even begin to tell the full story. All the modern technology in the world won't keep destructive storms from plummeting rigs or tankers. Nor will it resolve routine mishaps that will spill crude into the water.

The potential for disaster, for the economic devastation of Florida, is great. "National security" would be weakened because our own nature-based economy in Florida would be harmed beyond repair.

The great blue river of a current will wash—as it always has—across the Florida Keys, and northward, along the southern Florida coast. It will be strong and sure, and no slick political rhetoric will dilute its energy. Whatever enters this current will be transported by it—including crude oil. Our complex reef system, already under great stress, will suffer yet a new insult, one it's unlikely to survive.

To argue an economic case "for" drilling requires a full telling of the larger truth. It's a truth that explorers and scientists and writers have known for centuries: what is upstream always flows down.

Bill Belleville has authored five books and over one thousand magazine articles and essays, and he has scripted and produced seven documentaries. His work has appeared in New York Times, Sierra, Audubon, Oxford America, Islands, *and on* PBS *and* NPR's "Living on Earth." *He has traveled widely for the Discovery Channel, including expeditions to Cuba, the White Sea of Russia, and the Galapagos Islands. His latest book is a collection of nature essays,* Salvaging the Real Florida: Lost and Found in the State of Dreams.

OASES IN A SEA OF SAND

FELICIA COLEMAN

AND

CHRISTOPHER KOENIG

A spring day at sea, flat calm, cerulean sky, flying fish skitter over the water's surface after a storm pitched forty-foot waves here a few days ago. The view is sweet, serene, a hundred miles from any point of land. But our interests lie 250 feet below in the Gulf of Mexico on a shotgun spray of bright white specks seen on the marine geologist's acoustic maps, specks we thought might be fissures seeping freshwater from underground aquifers into the sea. We wait while the crew positions the ship and lowers a camera, remotely operated from the vessel.

As the cable feeds out, we hover around a screen mounted in the ship's laboratory, silent as the camera falls through brightly-lit water, through the gray flocculent remnants of the storm, and lands on the bottom, kicking up a cloud of sand. The umbilical cable lets the operator, a young man proficient with a joy stick, move the camera in a broad arc over the sea floor. Clusters of cone-shaped depressions, roughly one per acre, sprout up in bands across the bottom of the Gulf.

Slowly, as the camera beads in on the site, the bright speck from the map transforms into a swarm of fish. Closer, and the fish scatter to reveal a cone-shaped pit, fifteen feet wide, six feet deep. Closer, and the camera reveals rocks at the cone's center as well as scattered in its walls, formed millennia ago by the incursion of fresh water that no longer flows here. Absent is the telltale shimmer of less-dense water rising through its saltier surroundings. The cone becomes the focus, now, embedded in the hard bottom of the West Florida Shelf, a solution hole. It is surrounded by a thick lens of rounded sand particles formed by the calcareous skeletons of billions of plants and animals—algae, coral, sponges, mollusks—tumbling over the bottom, layered deeper and deeper over thousands of years.

On the surface of the rocks are carpets of coralline algae, bright red and pink, scores of organisms known to be marine animals, but seeming more like whimsical art forms—sea fans, sea whips, white splashes of coral clusters. Swimming about the interstices of the rocky gallery are small fish (rough-tongued bass, greenband wrasses, yellowtail reeffish) then larger fish (vermilion snapper, red porgy, triggerfish) and finally, one solitary, sedentary fish who seems to own the landscape, a male red grouper.

This fish sits quietly for hours until a female enters the cone. We sit in front of our screen, on our boat, watching. The two red grouper flash at each other in recognition. The male's head turns jet black as pearlescent lines radiate back from the eyes onto his black back, and the female develops several broad black and white vertical bars on her sides. Their *pas de deux* is swift, as they swim over the cone and then up off the bottom releasing egg and sperm. The near transparent cloud rises, drifts; small fish dart back and forth nervously through it, feeding on the fertilized eggs. The patterns on the grouper fade, the fish part. The female leaves. The male returns to the cone and drifts down to a rock, pectoral fins extended, mouth wide open in obvious display. A cleaner shrimp responds, moves into the grouper's mouth and out of the gills, picking bits of food, parasites, whatever morsels it can find. The display continues. A large reticulate moray eel approaches, glides its body across the fish's back, embracing the grouper again and again before disappearing into a crevice in the rocks.

The male grouper swims slowly around the inner wall of the cone, then drops to the bottom, scoops a mouthful of sand and swims some thirty feet away, outside of the cone, and purges the sand forcefully from its mouth, streaming the sand from the chambers that shield its gills. The fish repeats this pattern for nearly an hour and then returns to the rocks and sweeps the surface with its tailfin, temporarily suspending the sediment in the water column.

It is the cleaning behavior that intrigues us. Why does this fish move the sand? Why does any animal manipulate its space? For mates? For food? For shelter? This holy trinity of survival surely enters into the mix. The fish remind us of beavers, who build dams to protect themselves and their broods from predators and inclement weather. Yet these engineering feats have greater effects that extend beyond the architect's selfish needs, even extending beyond the boundaries of the manipulated space. The beaver's dam shelters other organisms, including migrating geese, and enhances the richness of plant life in surrounding meadows by interrupting the flow of water.

Red grouper, by cleaning these rocks, keep the solution holes from filling with sediments as bottom currents and storms surge over the seabed. They sweep them free of debris, exposing the surface for settling larvae to attach and transform into corals, sponges, and anemones. The rocks and attached sea creatures form a three-dimensional array of housing for the swimmers and walkers, thus a significantly more diverse community is centered within this cone and the next and the next embedded in the surrounding sand.

Removing the fish removes the architect, the engineer,

the maintainer, the driver of the community's diversity at the scale of the cone, clearly, and perhaps at a broader scale. As the young man pulls the camera back to the surface, and the fish, the rocks, the artistry all disappear from view, we imagine the cones filling slowly with sand.

As scientists, when we hear about proposals to drill for oil and gas in the Gulf of Mexico, the first question that comes to mind is, what are the ecological consequences? This question requires an answer.

The pressure to gather energy from the ocean is driven by a world population hungry for living and mineral resources. The living resources suffer from extraction at often unsustainable levels, while the mineral resources simply are finite, and their use the root cause of unprecedented changes in climate that threaten coastal regions globally.

Industry interests may present advanced technologies as if the outcome can be benign. The truth is, there is always a trade-off. Oil drilling, to a greater or lesser degree, disrupts natural ecological processes, and alters or reduces the ocean's ability to provide critical ecosystem services that help maintain life as we know it. As extractive activities move further offshore, they threaten even the deep sea, an area now known to provide the same kinds of ecosystem services as the coastal zone, now known to be as biologically diverse as tropical rainforests.

For a state that has already lost a significant portion of the structural habitat inshore—seagrass, saltmarsh, mangroves, coral, and oyster reef—that buffers the coast from storms and provides nursery habitat for fisheries species, nutrient cycling, and a myriad of other services, for a state whose Gulf Coast is one of the most biologically diverse and productive areas in the region, for a state that relies on these resources to support fisheries valued at $6 billion and tourism at $65 billion, how much more are its citizens willing to trade? This is the question each person must consider and to which each person must respond.

Dr. Felicia Coleman and Dr. Christopher Koenig are marine ecologists at the Florida State University Coastal and Marine Laboratory. They work in the eastern Gulf of Mexico on reef fishes and their habitat. Their recent studies include habitat engineering behaviors in red grouper, recovery of the critically endangered goliath grouper, and the function of shelf-edge no-take marine reserves in protecting reef fish spawning. Conservation through scientific understanding is the hallmark of their studies.

FLORIDA'S TEMPTRESS
WILLIAM F. HAMMOND

Grandpa used to say, "If you have to make a really tough decision, weigh all the options and choose the one that leaves you the most options for the future." That seems to have a profound application to the Florida decision about drilling for oil in the Gulf of Mexico.

Most of Florida's residents, both year-round and seasonal, live within a short drive to the beaches and estuaries that mix freshwater and seawater, forming one of nature's most perfect nurseries. Our sounds and shallow bays are fed by the solar rays that fuel the marine grasses, mangroves, salt marshes, macro algae, and microscopic phytoplankton all of which feed myriad marine creatures, many of whom then travel with tide and currents out into the Gulf to reproduce. Shrimp, fish, crabs, and clams send their seed and tiny offspring to grow offshore at the very time new generations of fish, whales, and other young predators come to the Gulf searching for the microscopic larvae, phytoplankton, and detritus in a rhythmic seasonal dance that has stretched from estuary to Gulf and back to estuary since the beginning of Florida's emergence from the last glacial era.

Given the clear need to conserve the unspoiled beauty of the Gulf, a beauty which lies at the heart of our tourist industry and thus our economy, it seems strange that some conservatives in the legislature seem to be the most vocal and vigorous supporters of the "drill, baby, drill!" campaign. Significantly, the political moderates from both parties, including conservationists and environmentalists, seem to be on the "no-drilling" side with a bent for saving Florida's unique environment. They support the protection and growth of the revenue that comes through tourism, fisheries, recreation and renewable energy development. This majority senses a way of life it feels is threatened by one "rare accident or mistake" or the incidental cumulative side effects of doing industrial business in the deep blue Gulf waters.

The vast majority of the spills, blowouts, and other impacting events, large or small, are linked to human error that always accompanies risky technological initiatives no matter how many redundant fail-safe technologies we employ. Placing oil rigs and pipelines in the coastal shelf waters, an environment prone to violent hurricane winds and storm-driven seas and tides, raises the risk for all coastal-water-based businesses and all marine, estuarine, and ecological systems. Should any type of spill happen, the Gulf Loop Current would sweep the slurry loaded with toxics along the entire Gulf Coast south to the Keys through the Florida Straits and up our East Coast beaches.

It is very hard to forget human error in the *Exxon Valdez* Alaskan oil spill, Three Mile Island and Chernobyl disasters, Santa Barbara oil spills, and the greatest Gulf drilling spill of them all, the Ixtoc event in 1979 just north of the coast of Mexico. Craig Pittman of the *St. Petersburg Times* chronicles, "that spill dumped more than 3 billion gallons of oil, caught fire and burned for a year hampering the capping process. Two months later the loop current delivered tar balls 600 miles away on the Texas coast." The claim that safety has improved substantially since that time is no doubt valid. But the small and moderate leaks and blowouts from oil rigs and service transportation that happen on a daily basis have become so common that only the very worst mistakes make the news. The rest pass quietly below the public view, but their secondary and cumulative impacts significantly degrade the environment and threaten both the ecological and economic vitality of our communities.

For more than a century, southwest Florida has been the state leader in harvest of finfish and shellfish because of its rich estuarine conditions of mangrove forests, seagrass, marine algae, and phytoplankton. These conditions make southwest Florida estuaries among the most productive in the world. The conversion of the sun's energy in the estuary works to earth-rhythms that have evolved in a ballet that performs to the changing seasons and patterns of rainfall and freshwater runoff. The estuarine link to the Gulf of Mexico provides an extremely productive form of both ecological and economic benefits.

If oil is a diminishing resource and our nation may have a critical need for it in the future, it remains safer in the ground while its value grows and scarcity and risk avoidance keeps our other energy resources valuable. Oil is simply stored sunshine and can be extracted from those leases off the coast in the Gulf if it ever does become an absolutely essential strategic resource. In the meantime, Florida legislators can push solar energy development and allow Florida to become a national industry leader in renewable energy development and production. As we emerge from this disastrous economic period, the buyer demand for "green" construction and design in buildings will be enormous. Energy efficiency in construction and electricity generation will become status quo, as will home solar recharging of plug-in electric vehicles, hybrids, and hydrogen cells that are already on the market.

Any thinking conservative politician or conservationist would conclude that Florida's rejection of drilling in the oil leases over the past decades is the prudent path to follow today. This decision is based upon a conservative economic plan that generates revenue and new capital investment in Florida's economy and keeps the liquid gold safely stored in the bank account in the substrate of the Gulf of Mexico as its value appreciates.

The Legislature would be well-served if they adopted grandfather's yardstick for judging success.

William F. Hammond is a professor emeritus of marine and ecological studies at Florida Gulf Coast University. Over the last fifty years, he has been an environmental educator in the public school system and at the university. He is President of Natural Context Consultants focused on environmental, creativity, education, and natural systems management, a national and international firm serving government, not-for-profit organizations, and corporate clients. Currently, he is special consultant to the Kitson & Partners Babcock Ranch Community, the world's largest solar-powered, smartest technological, and greenest community that preserves about 82,000 acres in public ownership as a wildlife preserve and working ranch.

LAST STAND

MATT SMITH

Florida stands out. A beacon and a redoubt, a defiant finger and a proffered hand, this place embodies unlike any other the riddles of peninsularity. We listen here for the first strains of the exotic, in the parrot's squawk, the coqui's clamor, the reggaeton beat—but also for the beleaguered howl of the native: the panther's scream, the ivorybill's rap, the Miccosukee's lilting tongue. The first beachhead in the conquest of the South, this land of sunshine—rising on the one hand, setting on the other—has become, improbably, a last stronghold of wildness.

Where that wildness clings on, in the sloughs of the Fakahatchee and the blue springs of the Ocala, stealing down the swales of Saint Vincent and slipping through the

Big Bend turtlegrass, it has done so by the grace of water. Mapped as hard land, a swatch as solid and crisp as its neighbors, Florida is in truth as ephemeral as Atlantis, risen from the waves, cradled and nursed and suffused by the sea, and condemned to rejoin it. In a kayak on the Aucilla or a skiff off the Tortugas, one can feel it. To enter the water, here, is not to confront something passive, something marginal. It is to enter a bloodstream, to pulse with a heart.

To treat the sea as passive and marginal is the first fallacy. To treat it as incorruptible, inexhaustible, is the second. Florida—where I have roots, though as shallow as an Australian pine's—has yet to feel the full consequences of both. To understand them, come with me to Mississippi, where I live now.

Here, you're too late. Your granddaddy's granddaddy might have seen a thing or two. Pine woods rolling like a flower-strewn sea, canebrakes you could fight through for days. Bison herds thundering over seashell prairie, hooves stained red from wild strawberries. Parakeets swirling down the bayou, red wolves cackling round your campfire. All that is gone. We paved it over with landscapes of our own invention: the asphalt sea, the soybean prairie, the dark and barren pulp-tree woods. Beneath them lies not only a defeated land, but a buried history, a history of exhaustion.

But what if I were to tell you of something else, a secret place, beyond the reach of the skidder and the combine and the backhoe? A place where the eagles still wheel and gnarled pines strain against the wind, and the green turtles heave themselves from the surf, just as they did for the frigates of Iberville? A place where you can still watch the galaxy whirl overhead, and listen to the sand shuffle itself underfoot, and lose your mind from the snarl of civilized life? What would such a place be worth?

That question is not rhetorical. The place exists, a humped serpent of sand draped between the Mississippi Sound and the open Gulf, four humps clearing the waterline. These are four of the last unblemished pearls in the barrier-island necklace, longest in the world, which lines America.

Their remoteness has preserved their life: turtles grazing through undersea meadows, terns thronging on white-sand spits, dolphins in the passes, gators in the lagoons, songbirds raining from April skies. It has also preserved their mythology. The islands throng with stories, from the rum-runners of Smugglers' Cove to the buried gold of the Empress of Mexico, from the lighthouse keeper's ghost to the mad painter who laughed in the teeth of Hurricane Betsy. These, like the plover or the leatherback, are fragile too. Uprooted, they wither.

The islands owe their resilience to their ephemerality. They are living, breathing, moving things, fed by riverborne Appalachian quartz, chased westward by waves and wind, reshaped and resurfaced by the great storms. They wriggle out from under lighthouses and strand them in the surf; they emerge and submerge like Brigadoon. And for over three centuries now, barely visible from shore as they slide along the horizon, they have continually slipped through the fingers of civilization. Two of them, Horn and Petit Bois, now boast national wilderness status, the most rigorous form of preservation we have. *This is what is left*, says the Wilderness Act, in one of the bravest and loveliest passages in our law. *Let it remain untrammeled by man.*

And this is what has happened since. Channel dredges, clearing the way for millions of barrels of crude each year to feed the giant refinery at Pascagoula, have shunted vast amounts of sand far offshore. Horn has lost a quarter of its land; Ship, a staggering two-thirds. This year's maps will be obsolete by next, as the waves eat away at the spits and bars, bringing nothing in return. Meanwhile, oil and gas leases were sold in the nearest fair-game federal waters, three miles from Horn. Appetites were whetted. State waters come nearer still; a law that absolved environmental authorities of their leasing responsibilities, and moved public hearings three hours inland, freed them for exploitation. The wilderness boundary itself remained the islands' last buffer, until a federal amendment, tucked into a military spending bill, rendered it porous to the point of disintegration. Seismic surveying immediately off the islands, and directional drilling beneath them, do not count as trammeling by man.

So now we are free to crowd the horizon with rigs, leaking their noxious metals and their storm-tossed slicks; we are free to bombard the sea with explosives, until we drive off everything within earshot; we are free to suck fuel from the islands' underbellies until they collapse. We may gain something, a few drops in the proverbial bucket. We may also be—perhaps we already are—answerable for a hideous crime, the final betrayal of that which made us what we are, the broken, besieged, exhausted, humiliated land.

For thousands of years, Mississippi's fugitive islands have found strength in fluidity, sliding and merging and dissolving like amoebae, yielding gracefully to winds and currents too stiff to resist. Now, hemmed in on all sides, they may have run out of moves.

But in Florida, you still have the luxury of choice. You will be told, as we all have, that your duty to these wild places is fully compatible (to the best of our knowledge, so reads the fine print) with the wise use of resources. What does this mean? That it is worth accepting a small risk, a risk to nature, for the sake of maintaining business as usual. On its own, such an argument is seductive. But we are distractible creatures, our memories delicate and short. The next time we are asked to take such a risk, we will have learned to live with the consequences of the last.

As our wild places ail—and they will, as long as our love lags our appetite—our baselines drift. Already, these places are fewer and farther between than ever, crumbling like sand, slipping beneath the tide. And still we are hungry.

Matt Smith, a writer, geographer and naturalist, spent three years enjoying the incomparable landscape of the Florida Panhandle. He now lives in his native city of Jackson, Mississippi, where he works at the Mississippi Museum of Natural Science and is pursuing an MFA in writing for children. His writing has most recently appeared in Bartram's Living Legacy: The Travels and the Nature of the South, *an anthology of essays on the naturalist William Bartram.*

THE VIEW FROM CEDAR KEY
LOLA HASKINS

There are acts we shouldn't risk,
the way we'd not send our children
across busy streets alone.

Perhaps nothing of ours would slick
the Gulf, no black goo coat
the feathers of staggering

birds, nothing clot the sand
toddlers love to mound. Perhaps
we'll never wake

to brown beaches. But what if we did?
I think of Cedar Key and
fine days kayaking

against the wind. And I remember
how it felt to land on
the farthest scrub

and know that the Gulf stretched
to Texas and Mexico but none
of its despoliation

bore our name. I ask you:
what is it worth to drive a mile
a penny cheaper?

I say not this. I say there are
places best left holy. I say
that if, when the money

is clamoring around us we
do not yield, then they will
come. And they will lie down

on our white sands and
remark to each other, shading
their eyes, how beautiful

this Florida is. And we
will smile inside, knowing
how gladly we paid the price,

and think *Yes, beautiful.*

Lola Haskins' tenth poetry collection, Still the Mountain, *is due in 2010, as is* Wild Angels, *stories from fifteen Florida cemeteries. Her prose work includes environmental essays and a poetry advice book. For more information, please see http://www.lolahaskins.com.*

ACKNOWLEDGEMENTS

Thank you to the Heart of the Earth Council, best of companions, always imagining how to create a shift in our culture that would make the thought of drilling for oil in the Gulf of Mexico irrelevant: Doug Alderson, Tom Anderson, Mike Brezin, Norine Cardea, Jeff Chanton, Barry Fraser, Cyndi Hunt, Mary Beth McBride, David Moynahan, Crystal Wakoa, and Lucy Ann Walker-Fraser.

We offer our heartfelt gratitude to the writers who contributed freely and beautifully to this book. May their voices ring in the cultural sea change we all long for.

Working with Lou Cross and David Moynahan on the creative design, production, and distribution of this book was a joyful and exciting collaboration, as always. They are immensely talented and their generosity is vast.

Special thanks to Charlie Hardee for his deep concern and good thinking about this project. Thanks for creative brainstorming to Julie Hauserman, Bob Rackleff, Jack Winchester, Roberta Isleib, Heidi Recksiek, and Glenn Sharron. Our deep appreciation goes to Tallahassee attorney Robert Rivas for wise counsel and a close reading of *Unspoiled*, and to our copy editor and dear friend Leeann Culbreath. Nicolette Lucia Costantino helped us type and put together the manuscript—we thank her so much.

Thank you to Stephen Trimble and Terry Tempest Williams for their creation of *Testimony: Writers of the West Speak on Behalf of Utah Wilderness*. Their book served as our inspiration.

Every day, all over Florida, nonprofit grassroots activists advocate on behalf of an unspoiled Florida. They are our Davids to the Goliaths of special interests. Our deepest respect and gratitude to them.

Our partners made it possible for us to devote these months to *Unspoiled*. Without the support of Jeff Chanton, Raven Waters, and Sasha Linsin Wohlpart this book would not exist.

CONTRIBUTOR PERMISSIONS

Doug Alderson, "View from the Mound," Copyright 2010 by Doug Alderson. Printed with permission from the author.

Marty Ambrose, "I Dreamed of Florida," Copyright 2010 by Marty Ambrose. Printed with permission from the author.

Bill Belleville, "The Great Blue River," Copyright 2010 by Bill Belleville. Printed with permission from the author.

Erin Canter, "Once More to the Coast," Copyright 2010 by Erin Canter. Printed with permission from the author.

Susan Cerulean, "Mullet Run," Copyright 2010 by Susan Cerulean. Printed with permission from the author.

Felicia Coleman, "Oases in a Sea of Sand," Copyright 2010 by Felicia Coleman. Printed with permission from the authors.

Jan DeBlieu, "North Carolina Triumph" Copyright 2010 by Jan DeBlieu. This essay originally appeared in *Mother Jones*, September-October 2001, in different form. Printed with permission from the author.

Connie May Fowler, "Big Oil, Big Sin," Copyright 2010 by Connie May Fowler. Printed with permission from the author.

Thomas Hallock, "The Way of All Flesh," Copyright 2010 by Thomas Hallock. Printed with permission from the author.

William F. Hammond, "Florida's Temptress," Copyright 2010 by William F. Hammond. Printed with permission from the author.

Lola Haskins, "The View from Cedar Key," Copyright 2010 by Lola Haskins. Printed with permission from the author.

Julie Hauserman, "Florida Postcard," Copyright 2010 by Julie Hauserman. Printed with permission from the author.

Grace C. Jackson, "Gulf of Mexico," Copyright 2010 by Grace C. Jackson. Printed with permission from the authors.

Jeff Klinkenberg, "Stormy Beach," Copyright 2010 by Jeff Klinkenberg. This essay previously appeared in the St. Petersburg Times and in *Pilgrim in the Land of Alligators: More Stories about Real Florida*, published by University Press of Florida (2008). Printed with permission from the author.

Christopher Koenig, "Oases in a Sea of Sand," Copyright 2010 by Christopher Koenig. Printed with permission from the author.

Ellie Alexandra Levy, "Drilling for Trouble," Copyright 2010 by Ellie Alexandra Levy. Printed with permission from the author.

Megan M. Melvin, "Head Above Water," Copyright 2010 by Megan M. Melvin. Printed with permission from the author.

Myra Mendible, "A Feral Beauty," Copyright 2010 by Myra Mendible. Printed with permission from the author.

Jono Miller, "What Florida Then?" Copyright 2010 by Jono Miller. Printed with permission from the author.

O. Victor Miller, *"Ichthus,"* Copyright 2010 by O. Victor Miller. Printed with permission from the author.

Jesse Millner, "Sanibel Island," Copyright 2010 by Jesse Millner. Printed with permission from the author.

Julie Morris, "Nearshore," Copyright 2010 by Julie Morris. Printed with permission from the author.

Riki Ott, "Beware the Sirens of Big Oil," Copyright 2010 by Riki Ott. Essay originally appeared in huffingtonpost.com on September 25, 2009. Reprinted with permission from the author.

Oannes Arthur Pritzker, "Ganawenia Nimamainan Aki," Copyright 2010 by Oannes Arthur Pritzker. Printed with permission from the author.

Dawn Evans Radford, "Keeping Watch," Copyright 2010 by Dawn Evans Radford. Printed with permission from the author.

Mandie Rainwater, "The Gulf of Generations," Copyright 2010 by Mandie Rainwater. Printed with permission from the author.

Janisse Ray, "First Landfall," Copyright 2010 by Janisse Ray. Printed with permission from the author.

Diane Roberts, "Selling Florida," Copyright 2010 by Diane Roberts. Printed with permission from the author.

Jack Rudloe, "Living from the Gulf," Copyright 2010 by Jack Rudloe. Printed with permission from the author.

Michael Savarese, "The Science of Climate Change in the Ten Thousand Islands," Copyright 2010 by Michael Savarese. Printed with permission from the authors.

Matt Smith, "Last Stand," Copyright 2010 by Matt Smith. Printed with permission from the author.

Linda Taylor, "The Soul of the Gulf," Copyright 2010 by Linda Taylor. Printed with permission from the author.

Crystal Wakoa, "The Shining Gulf," Copyright 2010 by Crystal Wakoa. Printed with permission from the author.

Jessica Wheeler, "Pricing the Priceless," Copyright 2010 by Jessica Wheeler. Printed with permission from the author.

A. James Wohlpart, "Sanctuary," Copyright 2010 by A. James Wohlpart. Printed with permission from the author.

Kathryn Keene Wohlpart, "Islands of Freedom," Copyright 2010 by Kathryn Keene Wohlpart. Printed with permission from the author.

Sasha Linsin Wohlpart, "The Science of Climate Change in the Ten Thousand Islands," Copyright 2010 by Sasha Linsin Wohlpart. Printed with permission from the authors.

Edward C. Woodward, "Patience at the Pass," Copyright 2010 by Edward C. Woodward. Printed with permission from the author.

ABOUT THE ARTIST

David Moynahan is a Florida conservation photographer and artist who lives in Wakulla County. His work has been widely used to help raise awareness and promote protection of Florida's remaining natural beauty through numerous organizations and projects, including Florida Fish and Wildlife Conservation Commission's Office of Recreation Services, Florida Wildlife *Magazine,* Trust for Public Lands, Legacy Institute for Nature and Culture, The Wildlife Society *of Florida, and our local environmental group,* Heart of the Earth. *David's work has received honors in many photo contests including those of the North American Nature Photographers Association and The Nature Conservancy, and his photos have been published in several calendars including the 2010 Florida Forever calendar and the 2010 Nature Conservancy Calendar. David Moynahan is committed to promoting the conservation of our state's natural heritage. Please visit http://www.davidmoynahan.com/ to enjoy more of his work.*

ABOUT THE DESIGNER

Lou Cross is designer and cartographer at Florida State University, and Creative Director with TSG Graphic Design in Tallahassee, Florida. His work can be found in a variety of publications, including the book, Between Two Rivers: Stories from the Red Hills to the Gulf (2004), *the* Recreation Guide to Florida's State Forests, *and the* Big Bend Saltwater Paddling Trail Guide. *His most recent project is an atlas of Florida's biodiversity to be published in conjunction with Florida Natural Areas Inventory. He is a valued and respected colleague to many for his creative vision and boundless generosity.*

Red Hills **Writers Project**
A Heart of the Earth Initiative

We are a local group of writers and editors who believe in the power of nature-based anthologies, poetry and memoirs to move and inspire people, and deepen their understanding of and attachment to place. This project is an initiative of the Heart of the Earth.

In our first publication, *Between Two Rivers: Stories From the Red Hills to the Gulf*, we draw on our region's storytelling tradition, hoping to boost local commitment to the ecological and cultural heritage of the Red Hills and Coastal Lowlands bioregions through the literary arts.

www.redhillswritersproject.org

the
Center for
Environmental
&Sustainability
Education
of FLORIDA GULF COAST UNIVERSITY

Publication of this book was made possible in part by a subvention from the Center for Environmental and Sustainability Education at Florida Gulf Coast University. The Center works toward realizing the dream of a sustainable and peaceful future for Earth through scholarship, education, and action. It advances understanding and achievement of the goals of environmental and sustainability education through innovative educational research methods, emergent eco-pedagogies, and educational philosophy and practice based on an ethics of care and sustainability.

www.fgcu.edu/cese

Heart *of the* Earth

Heart of the Earth is a movement fostering practical action to live more sustainable lifestyles within the context of the Red Hills and Gulf Coast Lowlands Bioregions, motivated and sustained by our spiritual connection to the Earth.

We encourage our members and friends to join us in personal pledges to reduce fossil fuel use by 30 percent within 36 months, and to investigate how to conduct our lives if we imagine ourselves truly native to this place. In support of these pledges, through memberships, community-building, educational workshops, discussion groups, newsletters and our web site, Heart of the Earth offers effective, science-based and doable solutions to the problem of global warming.

We enter into this work fired by the urgencies facing our planet and our growing understanding of the impact of our human actions: that we, as North Americans, are only among 25 percent of the world's population, but consume more than 70 percent of the world's resources and eat more than 60 percent of its food.

We believe that understanding the ecological gifts and constraints of our bioregion will allow us to develop effective and sustainable strategies so that all of us—human and nonhuman—may continue to live here.

www.heartoftheearth.org

Unspoiled. Writers Speak for Florida's Coast

Keep Florida's Coast